Economics
for Cambridge IGCSE™ and O Level

WORKBOOK

Susan Grant and Colin Bamford

Third edition with Digital access

Shaftesbury Road, Cambridge CB2 8EA, United Kingdom

One Liberty Plaza, 20th Floor, New York, NY 10006, USA

477 Williamstown Road, Port Melbourne, VIC 3207, Australia

314–321, 3rd Floor, Plot 3, Splendor Forum, Jasola District Centre, New Delhi – 110025, India

103 Penang Road, #05–06/07, Visioncrest Commercial, Singapore 238467

Cambridge University Press & Assessment is a department of the University of Cambridge.

We share the University's mission to contribute to society through the pursuit of education, learning and research at the highest international levels of excellence.

www.cambridge.org
Information on this title: www.cambridge.org/9781009814621

© Cambridge University Press & Assessment 2025

This publication is in copyright. Subject to statutory exception and to the provisions of relevant collective licensing agreements, no reproduction of any part may take place without the written permission of Cambridge University Press & Assessment.

First published 2014
Second edition 2018
Third edition 2025

20 19 18 17 16 15 14 13 12 11 10 9 8 7 6 5

Printed in the Netherlands by Wilco BV

A catalogue record for this publication is available from the British Library

ISBN   978-1-009-81462-1   Workbook with Digital Access

Additional resources for this publication at www.cambridge.org/9781009814621

Cambridge University Press & Assessment has no responsibility for the persistence or accuracy of URLs for external or third-party internet websites referred to in this publication and does not guarantee that any content on such websites is, or will remain, accurate or appropriate.

For EU product safety concerns, contact us at Calle de José Abascal, 56, 1°, 28003 Madrid, Spain, or email eugpsr@cambridge.org

Page/Getty Images.
Cover image: Eugene Mymrin/Getty Images
Section 2 Practice Question, Figure 1: Data from China Association of Automobile Manufacturers

> Endorsement

Endorsement indicates that a resource has passed Cambridge International Education's rigorous quality-assurance process and is suitable to support the delivery of their syllabus. However, endorsed resources are not the only suitable materials available to support teaching and learning, and are not essential to achieve the qualification. For the full list of endorsed resources to support this syllabus, visit www.cambridgeinternational.org/endorsed-resources

Any example answers to questions taken from practice questions, accompanying marks and mark schemes included in this resource have been written by the authors and are for guidance only. They do not replicate examination papers. In examinations the way marks are awarded may be different. Any references to assessment and/or assessment preparation are the publisher's interpretation of the syllabus requirements. Examiners will not use endorsed resources as a source of material for any assessment set by Cambridge International Education.

While the publishers have made every attempt to ensure that advice on the qualification and its assessment is accurate, the official syllabus, specimen assessment materials and any associated assessment guidance materials produced by the awarding body are the only authoritative source of information and should always be referred to for definitive guidance.

Our approach is to provide teachers with access to a wide range of high-quality resources that suit different styles and types of teaching and learning.

For more information about the endorsement process, please visit www.cambridgeinternational.org/endorsed-resources

Cambridge International Education material in this publication is reproduced under licence and remains the intellectual property of Cambridge University Press & Assessment.

Third-party websites and resources referred to in this publication are not endorsed.

2024 Cambridge Dedicated Teacher Awards

Our **Cambridge Dedicated Teacher Awards** are an opportunity to show appreciation for the incredible work teachers do every day.

Thank you to everyone who nominated this year; we have been inspired and moved by all of your stories. Well done to all of our nominees for your dedication to learning and for inspiring the next generation of thinkers, leaders and innovators.

Congratulations to our winners!

Global Winner
Southeast Asia & Pacific
Sydney Engelbert
Keningau Vocational College, Malaysia

East Asia
Pengfei Jiang
Zhuji Ronghuai Foreign Language School, China

Pakistan
Saeeda Salim
SISA - School of International Studies in Sciences & Arts, Pakistan

South Asia
Meena Mishra
Dr Sarvepalli Radhakrishnan International School, India

Middle East and North Africa
Gina Justus
Our Own English High school Sharjah-Girls, United Arab Emirates

Sub-Saharan Africa
Tajudeen Odufeso
Isara Secondary School, Nigeria

Europe
Aynur Bayazit
Menekşe Ahmet Yalçınkaya Kindergarten, Türkiye

Latin America & the Caribbean
Ramon Majé Floriano
Montessori sede San Francisco, Colombia

North America
Maria Medvetz Santos
Seminole Ridge Community High School, United States

For more information about our dedicated teachers and their stories, go to dedicatedteacher.cambridge.org

Contents

How to use this series		vi
How to use this book		vii
Introduction		ix
Developing skills		xi

1 The basic economic problem — 1

- 1 The nature of the basic economic problem — 2
- 2 Factors of production — 6
- 3 Opportunity cost — 10
- 4 Production possibility curve diagrams — 13

Section 1 practice questions — 17

2 The allocation of resources — 21

- 5 The role of markets in allocating resources — 22
- 6 Demand — 25
- 7 Supply — 31
- 8 Price determination — 35
- 9 Price changes — 40
- 10 Price elasticity of demand (PED) — 44
- 11 Price elasticity of supply (PES) — 49
- 12 Market economic system — 53
- 13 Market failure — 56
- 14 Mixed economic system — 60

Section 2 practice questions — 65

3 Microeconomic decision-makers — 71

- 15 Money and banking — 72
- 16 Households — 75
- 17 Workers — 78
- 18 Firms — 84
- 19 Firms and production — 89
- 20 Firms' costs, revenue and objectives — 93
- 21 Types of markets — 99

Section 3 practice questions — 103

4 Government and the macroeconomy — 109

- 22 Government macroeconomic intervention — 110
- 23 Fiscal policy — 113
- 24 Monetary policy — 118
- 25 Supply-side policy — 121
- 26 Economic growth — 125
- 27 Employment and unemployment — 128
- 28 Inflation — 133

Section 4 practice questions — 137

5 Economic development — 143

- 29 Living standards — 144
- 30 Poverty — 148
- 31 Population — 152
- 32 Differences in economic development between countries — 156

Section 5 practice questions — 160

6 International trade and globalisation — 167

- 33 Specialisation and free trade — 168
- 34 Globalisation and trade restrictions — 171
- 35 Foreign exchange rates — 175
- 36 Current account of the balance of payments — 180

Section 6 practice questions — 186

CAMBRIDGE IGCSE™ AND O LEVEL ECONOMICS: WORKBOOK

> How to use this series

This suite of resources supports students and teachers following the Cambridge IGCSE™, IGCSE (9–1) and O Level Economics syllabuses (0455/0987/2281) for examination from 2027. All of the components in the series are designed to work together and help students develop the necessary knowledge and skills for this subject.

The Coursebook is designed for students to use in class with guidance from the teacher. It offers complete coverage of the Cambridge IGCSE™, IGCSE (9–1) and O Level Economics syllabuses (0455/0987/2281). The Coursebook contains in-depth explanations of economics concepts, a variety of independent and group activities, engaging new features and images to help students make real-world connections.

A digital version of the Coursebook is included with the print version, and available separately. It includes access to video content to further support students' learning, as well as simple tools for students to use in class or for self-study.

The Workbook provides further practice of all the skills presented in the Coursebook and is ideal for use in class or as homework. It provides engaging activities, worked examples and opportunities for students to evaluate sample answers so they can put into practice what they have learnt.

A digital version of the Workbook is included with the print version. It includes simple tools for students to use in class or for self-study, as well as downloadable templates to complete some of the activities.

The Digital Teacher's Resource provides everything teachers need to deliver the course. It is packed full of useful teaching notes and lesson ideas, with suggestions for differentiation to support and challenge students, ideas for formative assessment, overcoming common misconceptions and language support.

The Digital Teacher's Resource contains downloadable resource sheets and worksheets.

All answers are available on Cambridge GO.

> How to use this book

Throughout this workbook, you will notice recurring features that are designed to help your learning. Here is a brief overview of what you will find.

LEARNING INTENTIONS

Learning intentions open each chapter. These help you with navigation through the Workbook and indicate the important concepts in each topic. The learning intentions also map to the content in the Cambridge IGCSE™ and O Level Economics Coursebook.

KEY TERMS

These provide a reminder of the key terms that you need to recall for each chapter topic.

Key skills activities

These are scaffolded exercises which support your progression through your course and enable you to put into practice what you have learnt so far. The activities have been clearly linked to the key skills that you need for economics.

SELF-ASSESSMENT

- Self-assessments will give you an opportunity for you to assess your own work in relation to the learning intentions.

TIPS

Tips are provided throughout this Workbook to help with your learning. These provide you with additional guidance and advice.

End-of-chapter practice questions

Each chapter contains a set of multiple-choice questions. You can use these to assess the knowledge you have gained on this topic.

End-of-section practice questions

Each section ends with a set of more demanding questions that includes an extended case study. These can be used to assess what you have learnt across several chapters of the Workbook.

WORKED EXAMPLES

Worked examples provide you with sample answers to help you understand how to respond to questions using key skills.

Improve this answer

This offers you an opportunity to evaluate a sample answer to a question. Advice and guidance are provided to help you assess the answer.

> **YOUR CHALLENGE**
>
> After completing 'Improve this answer', you are then asked to apply the advice to your own answer.

› Introduction

This Workbook is designed to help you develop your understanding of economics, to build your skills and to enable you to assess your progress. It can be used in conjunction with the Cambridge IGCSE™ and O Level Economics Coursebook.

The Workbook begins by exploring how you can develop the skills of an economist. It is then divided into six sections which correspond to the sections of the syllabus and the Coursebook. Each section, in turn, is divided into several chapters and ends with case study practice questions. There is guidance on how to approach the questions and some worked examples.

Chapters 1–36 start with the learning intentions you are aiming to achieve, followed by a list of the key terms associated with the topic of the chapter. Every chapter includes a range of activities to develop key skills that will help you reinforce your learning in what we hope is an enjoyable way. You will have the opportunity of checking your understanding of some of the key economic terms by matching them with their definitions. Your understanding of the key economic terms will be strengthened by other activities including completing crosswords and wordsearches. Sentence completion activities require you to process what you have learned to find words that ensure the sentences make economic sense and to help you build up links between, for example, causes and effects.

Other skills you need to develop are to undertake calculations and to draw and interpret diagrams. You will have the opportunity to undertake a range of calculations linked to an activity such as completing a sudoku puzzle. There are several activities that will develop your confidence and technique connected to production possibility curve diagrams, demand and supply diagrams, and cost diagrams.

Your analytical and evaluative skills will be strengthened by activities that include completing flow diagrams, tables and mind maps. There are also activities where you can rearrange words and terms in a grid to show how they are connected.

Each chapter contains at least one tip and a self-assessment activity. The tips are designed to help you avoid common mistakes and to provide advice on how you can improve the quality of your work. The self-assessment activities provide you with the opportunity to reflect on how confident you are with your progress.

Each chapter finishes with a set of multiple-choice questions. These will help you to both check your understanding and to develop your question technique. You will find a total of 175 multiple-choice questions in the Workbook.

You can either tackle a chapter or section of the book once you have completed the corresponding section of your course, or you can choose to work through all the sections towards the end of the course.

As with the accompanying Coursebook, this book seeks to cover all the topics in the syllabus. The figures in the book shown as $ are US dollars.

We hope you find the activities in this book both interesting and useful. Studying economics can be fascinating and can provide benefits both to you and to society. Alfred Marshall, a famous British economist, wrote in 1885 that his objective was to send economists 'out into the world with cool heads but warm hearts, willing to give some at least of their best to grappling with the suffering around them; resolved not to rest content till they have done what in them lies to discover how far it is possible to open up to all the material means of a refined and noble life.' Much has happened since Marshall wrote this, but still, it remains a worthy objective.

In preparing this new edition, we would like to thank our editor, Susan Ross, for her very useful suggestions and help. All sample answers have been written by the authors.

Susan Grant and Colin Bamford

> Developing skills

The skills of an economist

Economists use a range of tools and skills to interpret economic issues and events, to explain these and to make recommendations on choices and policy measures. As you study economics, you will develop a number of these skills including the ability to:

- show knowledge and understanding of the subject
- interpret and draw diagrams
- interpret data which may be in the form of written information, statistical tables, diagrams and graphs
- carry out basic calculations
- use economic formulas and equations
- analyse economic issues and events
- evaluate economic choices and policy measures
- write in a clear manner, using economic concepts and terms.

The skills you will need

This section will help you develop the key skills of an economist. It supports the Cambridge IGCSE™ and O Level Economics syllabus. For this syllabus, the skills you will need to learn can be found in Table 1, which shows the syllabus assessment objectives.

Table 1: Assessment objectives

AO1 Knowledge and understanding	AO2 Analysis	AO3 Evaluation
- demonstrate knowledge and understanding of economic definitions, formulas, concepts and theories - use economic terminology.	- select, organise and interpret economics data and information - apply economic analysis to written, numerical, diagrammatic and graphical data - analyse economic issues, identifying and developing links and relationships.	- evaluate economic information, data and arguments, and recognise that economic decisions have uncertain outcomes.

The information in this section is taken from the Cambridge International Education syllabus. You should always refer to the appropriate syllabus document for the year of examination to confirm the details and for more information. The syllabus document is available on the website: www.cambridgeinternational.org.

Command words

Command words at the start of questions are there to help you know what is expected when you write your answer. For example, a question that says 'Define inflation' is not the same as 'Explain inflation' or one that says 'Discuss the effects of inflation'.

Table 2 contains nine command words that are used for Cambridge IGSCE and O Level Economics.

Table 2: Commonly used command words

Command word	What it means
Analyse	Examine in detail to show meaning, identify elements and the relationship between them.
Calculate	Work out from given facts, figures or information.
Define	Give precise meaning.
Describe	State the points of a topic / give characteristics and main features.
Discuss	Write about issue(s) or topic(s) in depth in a structured way.
Explain	Set out the purposes or reasons / make the relationships between things evident / provide why and/or how and support with relevant evidence.
Give	Produce an answer from a given source or recall/memory.
Identify	Name/select/recognise.
State	Express in clear terms.

The information in this section is taken from the Cambridge International Education syllabus. You should always refer to the appropriate syllabus document for the year of examination to confirm the details and for more information. The syllabus document is available on the website: www.cambridgeinternational.org.

Show knowledge and understanding

Knowledge and understanding of economic terms, concepts and topics is the first skill to be developed. It underpins analysis and evaluation. You are not able to analyse or evaluate something until you know and understand it. To start with, you will not be familiar with some of the terms in economics, but the more you use them, the more confident you will become.

Interpret diagrams

Diagrams need to be considered carefully. Check to see what is being shown on the axes. The vertical axis is the line that runs up and down and is sometimes referred to as the y axis. The horizontal axis, also called the x axis, runs from side to side.

Then check what is plotted on the diagram. Figure 1 shows how many chocolate bars firms are willing and able to sell at different prices. The line which plots the different quantities that firms will supply at different prices is known as a supply curve. The diagram shows that firms are willing and able to supply more chocolate bars, the higher the price. Economic theory supports this relationship. This is because a higher price is likely to increase the revenue that the firm will receive.

Developing skills

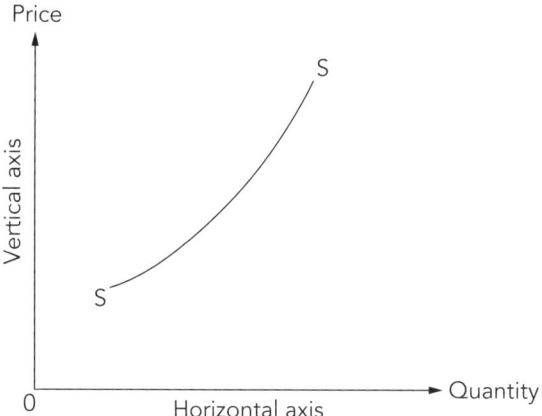

Figure 1: A supply curve showing how many chocolate bars firms are willing and able to sell at different prices

Draw diagrams

Diagrams are a key tool of an economist. They are used to analyse theories, predictions and relationships.

The main types of diagrams you may be required to draw are a demand and supply diagram, a production possibility curve diagram and diagrams of cost curves.

When drawing a diagram, it is important that you:

- use a ruler to draw the axes
- label the axes clearly and accurately, identifying the origin
- label the curves accurately
- make sure the diagram is large enough to be seen clearly
- explain what the diagram shows (unless you are asked just to draw a diagram).

Interpret data

Written data

You will come across a variety of forms of written data. These are likely to include passages from textbooks, newspaper articles and information on websites.

It is often useful to read through written data quickly the first time and then go back to read it more carefully.

Statistical tables

Statistical tables can be used to show and analyse changes in economic data and economic relationships, and to make comparisons between, for example, the behaviour of different households, firms and countries.

Table 2 shows data of the number of cans of soft drink that a firm has estimated it would be able to sell in a day at different prices. For example, it has estimated that it would be able to sell 30 cans if it charged $1, but only 20 cans if the price is $1.60.

Table 3: Number of cans of a soft drink that would be sold per day at different prices

Price of a can of soft drink ($)	Number of cans of soft drink that would be sold in a day
1.0	30
1.2	28
1.4	25
1.6	20
1.8	12
2.0	2

Question 1

Using Table 3, is the relationship between the price of the can and the number of cans sold the one you would expect? Explain your answer. Write the answer in your notebook.

TIP

Throughout this section, there are questions to help you develop the full range of skills that you will need to successfully start thinking like an economist. You could try answering them now or wait until you feel fully prepared.

Graphs

As with diagrams, it is important to check the axes carefully. They may be showing absolute figures or relative figures. For example, the vertical axis may be showing wage rates in dollars (absolute) or an index of wage rates (relative).

A graph may also be showing absolute figures or changes in those figures over time. For example, a graph may show a firm's total cost in different years or the change in its total cost over a period of time. Figure 2 shows the percentage change in a firm's total cost over a period of five years. Figure 3 shows the percentage change in a country's price level (the average of prices of goods and services in an economy) over the same period.

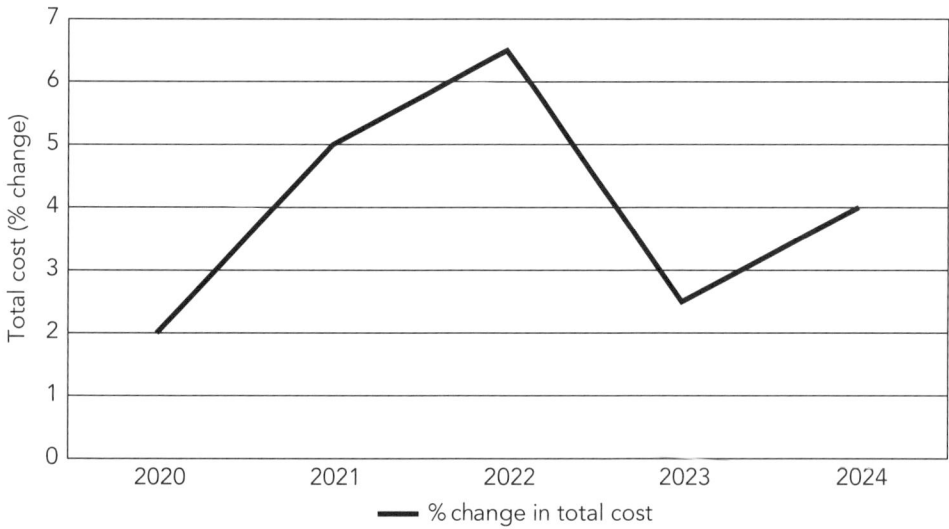

Figure 2: Percentage change in a firm's total cost, 2020–2024

Developing skills

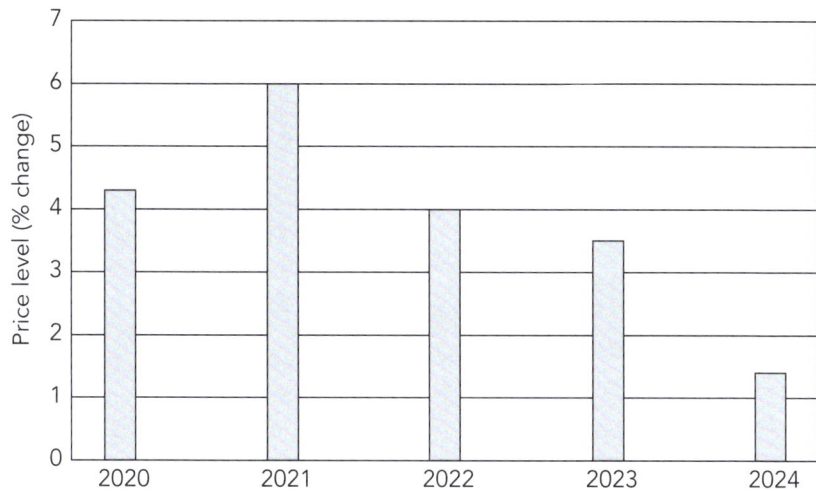

Figure 3: Percentage change in a country's price level, 2020–2024

Question 2

a Using Figure 2, explain what happened to the firm's total cost over the period shown.

b Using Figure 3, explain in which year the price level was highest.

Write the answers in your notebook.

Types of graphs

Economists use a wide range of graphs.

Time series line graphs

A time series line graph is commonly used. It plots one, or more, series of figures over a period of time. Figure 2 is an example of a time series line graph. A time series line graph may show trends. Figure 4, for example, shows that while the number of economics students in a school had an upward trend over the period 2020–2024, the number of geography students had a downward trend.

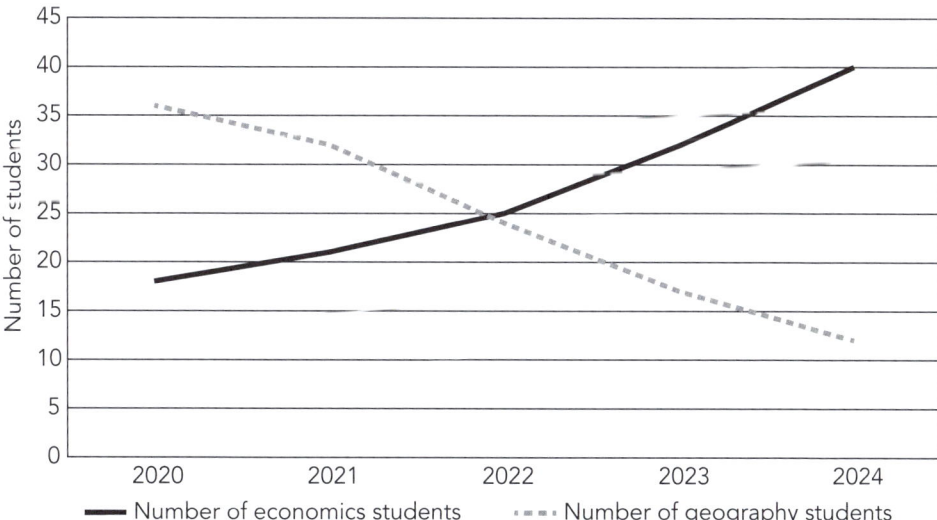

Figure 4: A school's economics and geography students, 2020–2024

Bar charts

Bar charts, such as Figure 5, show one or more bars either vertically or horizontally. The bars are used to compare data over a period of time or between different economic variables. The larger the height (in the case of vertical columns) or length (in the case of horizontal axes), the greater the relative size of the data. Figure 5 compares the number of people and the number of cars they have in each house in a street.

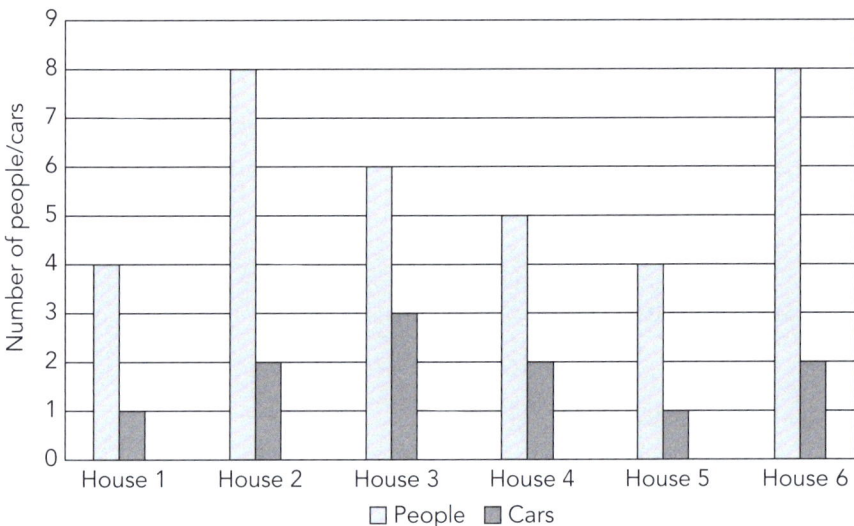

Figure 5: The number of people living in each house in a street and the number of cars owned by the occupants of each house

Pie charts

Pie charts are circular diagrams that are divided into segments, usually showing percentages. Figure 6 shows how a person spends a day.

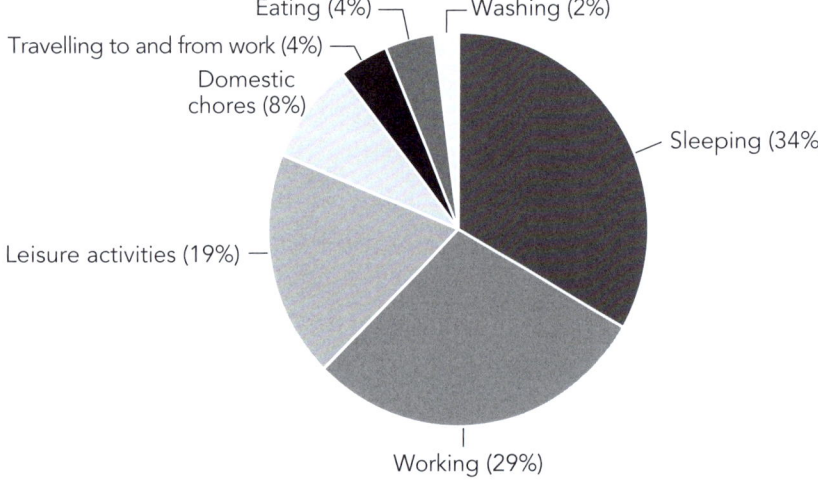

Figure 6: Use of hours in a day

Question 3

Using Figure 6, analyse the time the person spends on leisure activities, sleeping and working.

Scatter diagrams

A scatter diagram is used to see if there is a relationship between two variables. If there could be a line of best fit between the pair of variables that is upward sloping from left to right, it suggests a positive relationship between the two, with both moving in the same direction. If, on the other hand, there could be a downward sloping line of best fit, there may a negative relationship, with the variables moving in opposite directions.

Of course, it is possible that the pair of variables may be scattered randomly on the graph. This would indicate no relationship between the two variables. Figure 7 shows the hours students spend on revising, on average, per week and their success rates in passing examinations, with 0% indicating that they had failed all their subjects and 100% indicating that they had passed all their exams.

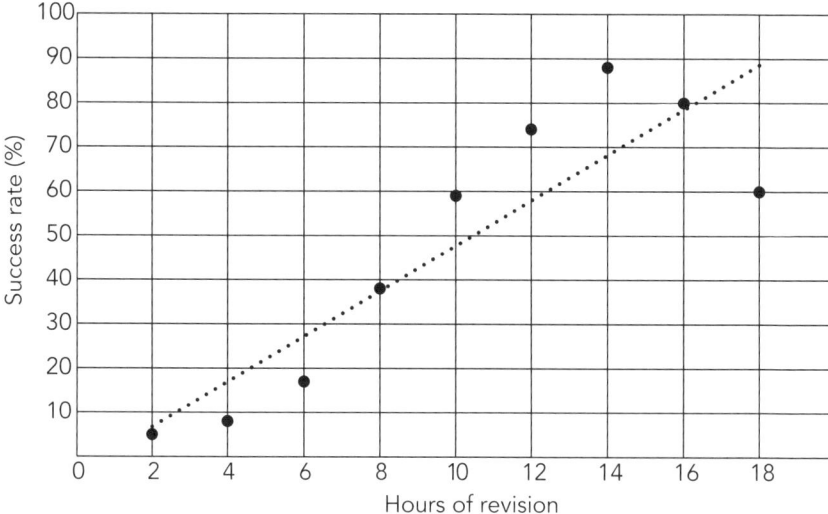

Figure 7: Success rate

Question 4

Analyse the relationship shown in Figure 7.

Carry out basic calculations

Economists interpret numerical data and carry out basic calculations. The numerical data that you might be expected to interpret could include index numbers, percentages and averages. The calculations could also include percentages, averages, multiplication, division, addition and subtraction.

It is important that you do not get confused between units, tens, hundreds, thousands, millions, billions and trillions. Table 4 shows the different sizes of numbers.

> **TIP**
>
> When carrying out a calculation, it is a good idea to show your working as to how you arrived at your answer. It is also good practice to consider whether the answer you have calculated looks right. For example, $90m would not look right as the income per head of a low-income country.

Table 4: Different sizes of numbers

Number		Number of 0s
One	1	0
Ten	10	1
Hundred	100	2
Thousand	1 000	3
Million	1 000 000	6
Billion	1 000 000 000	9
Trillion	1 000 000 000 000	12

Question 5

Carry out these calculations:

   a If five firms sell a product at $40, $45, $48, $50 and $57, what is the average price charged?

   b 60% of the 30 students in class A buy an economics textbook, and 50% of the 40 students in class B buy the book. What is the difference in the number of textbooks the two classes buy?

   c A football club played 40 matches. It won 22 and drew 13. What percentage did it lose?

   d A country has a total income of $500 billion (bn) and a population of 20 million (m). What is the income per head of the population (average income)?

Write the answers in your notebook.

Use economic formulas and equations

A good economist must be familiar with a number of formulas and equations, such as price elasticity of demand, price elasticity of supply, average total cost, average fixed cost, average variable cost, average revenue and real GDP per head.

Analyse economic issues and events

Analysis is built on knowledge and understanding. It involves explaining points, establishing links between points, applying economic concepts, interpreting data, using diagrams and undertaking calculations.

The key words to remember when you are seeking to establish analysis are 'why' and 'how'. For example, if you are asked to analyse the causes of a fall in the death rate and you identify an improvement in nutrition, you need to explain why this could have resulted in people living longer. The 'why' and 'how' parts of this economic issue are linked. This is what is meant by 'economic analysis'.

As you progress through the course, you will start to think like an economist. This involves thinking logically, analysing key economic issues, and considering causes and consequences. You will learn to apply economic theory and concepts to new situations.

One of the reasons why economics is highly regarded as an academic subject is because it develops the skill to think in a clear and reasoned way.

Evaluate economic choices and policy measures

Evaluation is the highest order skill. It builds on both knowledge and understanding and analysis. It involves assessing, for example, both sides of an argument, costs and benefits, possible different outcomes of a choice and the effectiveness of different government policy measures. An economist working for a government, for example, may be asked to set out the case both for raising the standard rate of income tax and for leaving it unchanged, and to explain which they would recommend. An economist working for a firm may be required to assess the advantages and disadvantages for the firm resulting from the introduction of a national minimum wage.

Structure of the assessment

There are two papers:

- Paper 1 is a multiple-choice paper with 40 questions.

- Paper 2 is designed to measure knowledge and understanding, analysis and evaluation. The paper has two sections. Section A consists of one question in six parts; and Section B contains four questions of which you must answer three.

- The information in this section is taken from the Cambridge International Education syllabus. You should always refer to the appropriate syllabus document for the year of examination to confirm the details and for more information. The syllabus document is available on the website: www.cambridgeinternational.org.

> **TIP**
>
> The most influential economists tend to be those who can write clearly. It is important that you write clearly so you can display your knowledge and understanding of the subject and show you can use economic concepts and terms to analyse and evaluate economic issues. It is also a good idea to write short sentences which make clear what you are writing about.

How the Workbook may help you develop and assess your knowledge and skills

The Workbook is designed to help you develop your knowledge of economics as you progress through the Cambridge IGCSE™ and O Level course. Working through the chapters will help you feel more confident about what you need to know to be a successful economics student.

Each chapter includes key skills activities and practice multiple-choice questions that will enable you to build up your skills and core knowledge of economics. At the start of the chapter, you will find a list of learning intentions. These outline the skills you will be expected to have developed by the end of the chapter.

The Workbook offers a wide range of key skills activities such as crosswords, wordsearches and sudoku. Other activities require you to put missing words into a phrase or sentence or to see if you can recognise the order of a sequence of economic events. Completing these activities will help you to know how well you are progressing with the content of each chapter. It is a good idea for you to keep a record of the activities you have done well and those where you have scope to improve. On completion of each chapter, we hope you will agree that economics really can be an interesting subject to study.

The 36 chapters are divided into six sections:

1 The basic economic problem
2 The allocation of resources
3 Microeconomic decision-makers
4 Government and the macroeconomy
5 Economic development
6 International trade and globalisation.

At the end of each section, there are two questions based on source material provided and two four-part questions. In addition, there are two worked example answers and two answers where there is an opportunity for you to write your own answer improving on what has been written.

Mind maps

When preparing for your examinations, it is good practice to use a mind map. This can help with your understanding of economics. A mind map is a diagram in which information is represented visually, usually with a central idea. Associated ideas are set out in branches extending from the centre. This is a good way of seeing how terms and topics fit together and is a useful way of planning an answer to a longer question. There is an example of a mind map activity in Chapter 27.

Multiple-choice questions

All multiple-choice questions (MCQs) in this resource consist of four possible responses, one of which is correct. There are various ways of arriving at the correct answer. Always read the question carefully, noting any key terms or hints as to what the question is asking such as 'likely', 'least likely', 'smallest' or 'largest'. Then:

- Cross out any responses that are clearly wrong.
- Look for any key terms in the question and in the responses.
- Choose the answer that makes most sense.
- Do not remain too long on any question.
- Make a guess if you are still unsure (as this is better than not answering the question).

Section 1
The basic economic problem

Chapter 1
The nature of the basic economic problem

LEARNING INTENTIONS

By the end of this chapter, you will be able to:

- define the basic economic problem
- explain the concept of scarcity
- give examples of the basic economic problem in the context of consumers, workers, producers/firms and governments
- explain the key resource allocation decisions answering the three basic economic questions of what to produce, how to produce and for who to produce
- explain the differences between economic goods and free goods.

KEY TERMS

resources   the basic economic problem   scarcity
economic good   free good

Key skills activities

1   Link each key term to its correct definition. An example has been done for you.

Term	Definition
The basic economic problem	A product that does not require resources to make it and so does not have an opportunity cost.
Economic good	A product which requires resources to produce it and therefore has an opportunity cost.
Free good	A situation where there are not enough resources to satisfy everyone's wants.
Resources	Unlimited wants are greater than finite resources.
Scarcity	Inputs used to produce goods and services.

1 The nature of the basic economic problem

2 Complete the sentences below using words from the box.

| basic economic problem   consumers   finite resources   governments |
| infinite wants   how   limited   producers   resources   scarcity |
| what   who |

a The .... has always existed as

.... have always been greater than ....

b There are not enough .... to meet everyone's wants.

c .... forces people to make choices.

d .... cannot buy everything they would like to because they have limited income.

e Workers have to decide what jobs to do as they have .... time.

f .... have to decide what to make and .... have to decide what to spend tax revenue on.

g Economies have to decide .... to produce, ... to produce and .... to produce for.

3 You are an employer who wants to hire an economist. Four people apply for the job. Each applicant claims to be an economist but only one is telling the truth. You ask each of the applicants to make a statement about the basic economic problem.

a Circle the statement made by the economist.

- Applicant A: Not all countries experience the basic economic problem.
- Applicant B: Countries have an unlimited supply of inputs.
- Applicant C: Countries' maximum output of goods and services is limited by the resources they have.
- Applicant D: Some countries experience very high prices, but the basic economic problem facing most countries is unemployment.

b Write an explanation to each of the unsuccessful applicants about what was wrong with their statement and an explanation to the successful applicant on why their statement was correct.

Write your answers in your notebook.

4 Two friends are invited to take part in a television programme called *Stranded* in which they need to survive on a desert island for a month. The island has an average of seven hours of sunshine a day and heavy rain twice a week. There is some fruit on the island and some lizards and tortoises.

The friends are allowed to take only **eight** items from the following list:

beans	hammock	sleeping bag
compass	insect repellent	solar-powered torch
cooking pot	pocketknife	sunscreen
first-aid kit	mirror	tent
fishing rod	mosquito net	water filter
football	rice	

a Which **eight** items would you take? Give reasons for your choice. You could discuss your choices with a partner.

b Explain how the activity illustrates the basic economic problem.

c Identify two free goods that you may be able to take advantage of.

Write your answers in your notebook.

> ### SELF-ASSESSMENT
>
> How confident did you feel after completing Activity 4? Think about the points below. Then circle the number of smiley faces to show your level of confidence from 1 (need to revisit my understanding of the basic economic problem) to 5 (feeling very confident).
>
> - Did you remember what is meant by the basic economic problem? Did you have to check the definition? What will you do to help you remember definitions of economics terms?
>
> - Would you have been able to explain why all the items on the list are economic goods and how economic goods differ from free goods?
>
>

> ### TIP
>
> In explaining the difference between economic goods and free goods, it is often useful to give examples.

Chapter 1 practice questions

Circle the correct answer to each question.

1   What would cause an increase in the problem of scarcity?

    A   A reduction in resources with wants unchanged

    B   A reduction in wants with resources unchanged

    C   A rise in the number of workers and no change in wants

    D   A rise in wants and a greater rise in resources   [1]

> **TIP**
>
> It's important to read questions carefully. You may find it helpful to highlight or underline key words in the question. You will need to think about your understanding of the word you have highlighted. For example, in question 1, you might highlight the word 'scarcity'. Then you will need to decide which one of the answer options is closest to your understanding of scarcity. Sometimes, you will need to consider the question along with the options. In question 2, you cannot decide on the answer until you have read the options.

2   Which form of air is an economic good?

    A   Air above an ocean

    B   Air at ground level

    C   Air from an air-conditioning system

    D   Air in a tropical rainforest   [1]

                                    Total: [2]

Chapter 2
Factors of production

LEARNING INTENTIONS

By the end of this chapter, you will be able to:

- define the factors of production: land, labour, capital and enterprise
- identify the rewards to the factors of production: rent, wages, interest and profit
- analyse the causes of changes in the quantity and quality of the factors of production.

KEY TERMS

capital   capital goods   consumption   consumer goods
depreciation   enterprise   entrepreneur   factors of production
gross investment   investment   labour   labour force
labour productivity   land   net investment
negative net investment   output   productivity

1   Link each key term to its correct definition. An example has been done for you.

Term
Capital goods
Consumer goods
Enterprise
Entrepreneur
Investment
Labour
Land

Definition
A person who takes the risks and makes the key decisions in a business.
Goods and services purchased by households for their own satisfaction.
Human effort used in production.
Artificial goods used in production.
Natural resources used in production.
Risk-taking and key decision-making in business.
Spending on capital goods used in production.

2 Table 2.1 shows different situations, the type of factor of production involved and an example of the factor of production. Complete the table. An example has been done for you.

Table 2.1: Factors of production used in different situations

Situation	Factor of production	Example
A firm producing orange juice increases its output.		Oranges
A cricket team decides to increase the number of people who can attend matches.	Capital	
Demand for gym membership increases.	Enterprise	More gyms set up
A TV series goes from once a week to three times a week and so has to employ more factors of production.	Labour	
A hospital expands to carry out more operations.		Operating theatres

SELF-ASSESSMENT

How confident did you feel completing Activity 2? Do you think you would be able to produce a table with different situations for another student to complete?

3 A small group of friends produce videos for social media. Table 2.2 lists some of the factors of production they employ. Identify each type of factor.

Table 2.2: Factors of production used in the production of videos

Factor of production	Type of factor
Camera operator	
Script writer	
Video camera	
Video editing software	
Place where video is filmed	
Director	
Person who paid for the equipment	

TIP

Remember that land in economics includes not just physical land but all natural resources.

4   All the words in the box are related to factors of production. See if you can find them in the wordsearch. You can download Worksheet 2.4 from GO to complete it.

| combine | entrepreneur | factors of production | human |
| innovate | organise | profit | risks |

5   You are running a paper manufacturing firm. It uses wood, water and machinery in the production of paper and employs 40 workers. You find that the quality of the capital, labour and land you employ has declined.

In your notebook, write down **one** possible reason for the decline in the quality of each of the factors of production and **one** way of improving each of the factors of production.

> **TIP**
>
> Remember that profit is the reward to the entrepreneur and not to capital.

Chapter 2 practice questions

Circle the correct answer to each question.

1   What is meant by 'investment in human capital'?

   A   Encouraging immigration of people of working age

   B   Paying bonuses to workers to encourage them to increase their output

   C   Spending money and time on educating and training workers

   D   Upgrading the machines labour works with   [1]

2   Which item is a factor of production?

   A   The food a farmer produces

   B   The satisfaction a farmer gains from their work

   C   The tractor a farmer drives

   D   The wages a farmer pays their workers   [1]

3   Which item used in the production of textiles by a firm would an economist classify as land?

   A   Sewing machines

   B   The factory

   C   Untrained workers

   D   Water taken from a river   [1]

4   What is meant by 'labour' in economics?

   A   Hard physical work used to produce manufactured goods

   B   Human mental and physical effort used in producing goods and services

   C   Natural resources used in the productive process

   D   Risk-taking and organising the factors of production [1]

5   Which type of factors of production are a football stadium and an owner of a football club?

	Football stadium	Owner of a football club
A	capital	entrepreneur
B	capital	labour
C	land	entrepreneur
D	land	labour

[1]

Total: [5]

> Chapter 3
Opportunity cost

> **LEARNING INTENTIONS**
>
> By the end of this chapter, you will be able to:
>
> - define opportunity cost
> - give examples of opportunity cost in different contexts
> - explain the influence of opportunity cost on decisions made by consumers, workers, producers/firms and governments when allocating their resources.

> **KEY TERM**
>
> opportunity cost

Key skills activities

1. You plan to attend an hour's revision session on one of these topics: the basic economic problem, factors of production or opportunity cost.

    a Which topic would you select to have the revision session on?

    b What might be the opportunity cost of selecting this choice?

    c What might be the opportunity cost of you attending this session?

    Write your answers in your notebook.

2. You are planning to go to a concert at the weekend. You have $30 to get there, and you would like to travel by taxi or car. It would cost $40 to travel by taxi, $30 by train and $15 by bus.

    a What is the opportunity cost of travelling to the concert by train?

    b How may the opportunity cost change if a friend offers to drive you there for $28 and you accept the offer?

    Write your answers in your notebook.

3. A farmer who grows carrots will have to take a range of decisions. Complete Table 3.1 with examples of some of these choices and their possible opportunity costs.

Table 3.1: Production choices and their possible opportunity cost

Decision	Choice	Possible opportunity cost
Which crop to grow?	Carrots	
Which factor of production to employ to increase to pick more carrots?		Capital
	Local supermarkets	A farm shop

> **TIP**
>
> At any one time, a choice we make will have an opportunity cost. However, do not think that the opportunity cost will always be the same one. Question 5 will help you think why the opportunity cost may change as circumstances change.

4   A government expects to receive $280bn in tax revenue. It actually receives $300bn. It is considering how to spend the extra $20bn. It narrows the choices to four: build a new hospital, build a new university, increase the pay of teachers, doctors and nurses, or improve the country's sea defences.

   Decide which of the four choices you would select. What do you think would be the opportunity cost? Write the reasons for your choices in your notebook.

5   Opportunity cost may change for a number of reasons. Complete Table 3.2 with reasons for change. The last one has been done for you.

Table 3.2: Changes in opportunity cost

Choice	Original opportunity cost	New opportunity cost	Reason for change
Purchase of an apple	Purchase of an orange	Purchase of a banana	
Production of accounts textbooks	Production of business textbooks	Production of economic textbooks	
Employment as an assistant in a bookshop	Employment as an assistant in a clothes shop	Employment as an assistant in a supermarket	
Government spending on education	Government spending on transport	Government spending on healthcare	Increase in number of older people in the population

> **SELF-ASSESSMENT**
>
> How confident did you feel completing Activity 5? Were you able to apply the concept of opportunity cost?
>
> Produce a revision card with a definition of opportunity cost and give three examples.

Chapter 3 practice questions

Circle the correct answer to each question.

1   What is meant by 'opportunity cost'?

   A   The best alternative forgone

   B   The cost of exploring business opportunities

   C   The cost of the item selected

   D   The labour used in producing the product   [1]

2   What might be the opportunity cost of using a bus to transport students to school?

   A   Increasing the revenue of the bus company

   B   Paying for the cost of petrol used

   C   Paying the wages to the driver

   D   Transporting a group of older people on a day out   [1]

3   Four firms can produce soap and perfume. The table below shows the maximum number of bars of soap and bottles of perfume that each firm can make each day if they specialise in one type of product.

	Bars of soap	Bottles of perfume
Firm W	50	10
Firm X	60	12
Firm Y	64	16
Firm Z	90	20

Which firm has the lowest opportunity cost of producing perfume?

A   Firm W

B   Firm X

C   Firm Y

D   Firm Z   [1]

4   What may be the opportunity cost of watching a concert?

A   The cost of the ticket

B   The cost of transport to the concert

C   The time spent at the concert

D   The time spent at an economics revision class   [1]

5   A firm can produce gloves and scarves. The table shows the combination of the two products it could make.

Pairs of gloves	Scarves
0	85
18	70
34	50
48	26
60	0

If the firm is currently producing 18 pairs of gloves and 70 scarves, what would be the opportunity cost of producing 16 more pairs of gloves?

A   15 scarves

B   20 scarves

C   50 scarves

D   85 scarves   [1]

Total: [5]

> Chapter 4
Production possibility curve diagrams

> **LEARNING INTENTIONS**
>
> By the end of this chapter, you will be able to:
> - define a production possibility curve (PPC)
> - draw a PPC
> - interpret points under, on and beyond a PPC
> - analyse movements along a PPC
> - analyse the causes and consequences of shifts in a PPC in terms of an economy's growth.

> **KEY TERM**
>
> **production possibility curve (PPC)**

Key skills activities

1   Economists make widespread use of diagrams. A diagram can be used to illustrate economic concepts, to analyse changes in economic conditions and to assess the effects of economic policies. Indeed a diagram can be worth a hundred words! Production possibility curve (PPC) diagrams can be used to show a number of economic concepts including opportunity cost.

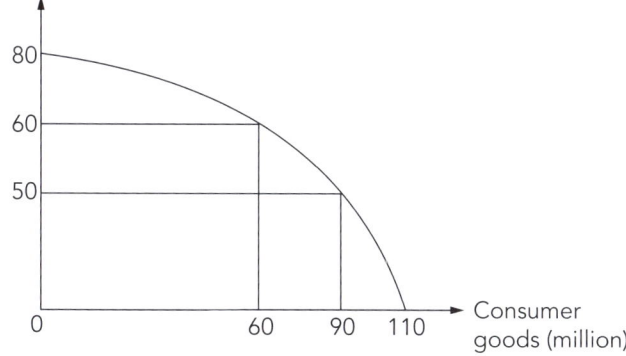

Figure 4.1: Different combinations of capital and consumer goods

Using Figure 4.1, state:

a   The opportunity cost of increasing the output of consumer goods from 60m to 90m consumer goods

b   The opportunity cost of producing 80m capital goods.

Write your answers in your notebook.

2   In Figure 4.2, AB is the original PPC.

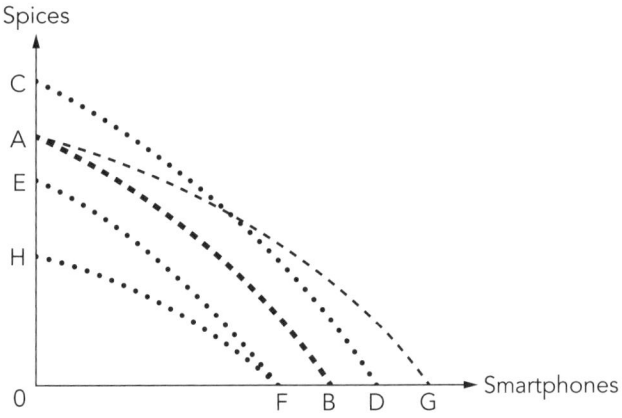

Figure 4.2: Production possibility curves

Decide which of the PPCs would match:

a   An increase in labour productivity

b   Advances in technology affecting the production of smartphones

c   A decrease in the size of the labour force

d   A heavy flood affecting large parts of the country.

Write your answers in your notebook.

3   Complete Table 4.1 to show how two concepts and one change can be shown on a PPC diagram.

Table 4.1: What a PPC diagram can show

Concepts/change	Shown on a PPC diagram
	The curve itself showing there is a limit to what can be produced with existing resources and technology.
Opportunity cost	
A change in the quantity of factors of production	

> **TIP**
>
> If it is appropriate to include a PPC diagram in an answer, you can draw a downward sloping line that touches both axes. This can be quicker to draw and may avoid you making the mistake of drawing the curve dipping down as it approaches the vertical axis.

4   A baker has two hours available to spend making bread rolls and mooncakes. Each roll and each mooncake sells for $1. Depending on how long the baker spends on making each product, the number of bread rolls and mooncakes produced is shown in Table 4.2.

Table 4.2: A baker's production decisions

Time spent making bread rolls (minutes)	Number of bread rolls produced	Time spent making mooncakes (minutes)	Number of mooncakes produced
20	18	20	20
40	34	40	30
60	40	60	38
80	45	80	45
100	48	100	48
120	49	120	50

a   Draw a PPC to show how the baker could allocate their time between making the two products.

b   Show on the PPC which allocation of time would result in the baker earning the most revenue.

Write your answers in your notebook.

> ### SELF-ASSESSMENT
>
> How confident did you feel completing Activity 4? Think about the points below.
>
> - Did you draw a straight, downward sloping PPC with a ruler?
> - You may have found b relatively tricky. The PPC allows you to illustrate the point which gives the best allocation of time. However, you have to work out first where this point will be found by using the figures in the table. Would you be able to explain to a partner how you decided on your answer to b?

Chapter 4 practice questions

Circle the correct answer to each question.

1   What does a production possibility curve (PPC) diagram show?

   A   The maximum combination of two types of products that can be produced with given resources

   B   The prices of two types of products being produced

   C   The quantity of capital and consumer goods that people would like to be produced

   D   The relative profitability of capital and consumer goods   [1]

2 Which combination of economic concepts is illustrated by a PPC?

   A Cost and price

   B Demand and price

   C Economic goods and free goods

   D Opportunity cost and scarcity [1]

3 What does a point outside a PPC represent?

   A A currently unattainable position

   B An inefficient position

   C The maximum use of resources

   D Unused resources [1]

4 Why may a PPC shift to the left but an economy's output of both types of goods increase?

   A The quantity of resources has decreased and greater use is made of the resources

   B The quantity of resources has decreased and there has been a movement up the PPC

   C The quantity of resources has increased and less use is made of resources

   D The quantity of resources has increased and there has been a movement down the PPC [1]

5 Why may Country Y have a PPC further to the right than Country Z?

   A Country Y has a higher quantity of land

   B Country Y has a higher rate of departure of enterprise to other countries

   C Country Z has a larger labour force

   D Country Z has a more productive labour force [1]

Total: [5]

Section 1 practice questions

1   Read the source material carefully before answering all parts of the question.

Pakistan fact file	2023
Population	248m
GDP per head	$5 200
Life expectancy	Male: 68 years
	Female: 72 years

Healthcare for Pakistan's population is through a mixture of government and private provision. The government provides just under half of all services. These services are paid for through various taxes and other charges on consumers and businesses. Most of these services are free of charge to patients. Just over half of healthcare services are provided through privately owned businesses, most of which are small. Private treatments are charged on a 'fee for service' basis. The quality of all services tends to be better in Pakistan's cities when compared to rural areas. An estimated 70% of the population receives some treatment from private businesses. The generally held view is that the private businesses outperform the government's services in terms of service quality and public satisfaction.

Table 1: Government spending on healthcare, 2022 and 2023

	Dollars $ ('000m)
Total government spending on healthcare (2022)	8.06m
Total government spending on healthcare (2023)	8.68m
Types of government spending on healthcare (2023):	
Hospital services	5.90m
Other: Public health services	1.10m
Administration	1.60m
Medical equipment	0.15m
Public Sector Development Programme (PSDP)	4.70m

The government's financial contribution to healthcare is shown in Table 1. The largest sum is spent on hospital services. More modest amounts are allocated for services such as nurses and doctors at local health centres and for operating theatres in hospitals. In addition, the government has allocated the substantial sum of $4.7('000m) for new improvement schemes. These schemes come under the Public Sector Development Programme (PSDP) and are designed to build new, state-of-the-art hospitals to enhance the quality of treatments available through government healthcare.

A key issue is that Pakistan's population has been growing at a faster rate than the growth in healthcare funding. The government's contribution to healthcare was 1.4% of GDP in 2023. This is less than the 5%–6% of GDP recommended by the World Health Organisation. The basic economic problem is that if the government allocates more funding for healthcare, less resources will be available for other areas of government spending such as education.

Refer to the information in the source material in your answers.

a Calculate the percentage change in government spending on healthcare from 2022 to 2023. [2]

b Identify **two** factors of production in the provision of healthcare in Pakistan. [2]

c Explain why healthcare in Pakistan is an economic good. [2]

d Explain **two** ways in which opportunity cost can be applied to healthcare spending decisions in Pakistan. [4]

e The Pakistan government is trying to decide whether to spend more on education and less on healthcare. Using a production possibility curve (PPC) diagram, analyse how opportunity cost applies if more resources are used for education. [4]

f Discuss whether or not the Pakistan government should increase its expenditure on healthcare above the current level of 1.4% GDP. [6]

Total: [20]

WORKED EXAMPLE FOR PART D

The Pakistan government is facing a situation where its population has been growing at a faster rate than it has been able to fund healthcare. There is a need to increase healthcare funding, but if this happens, some other area of government spending will have its funding cut back. The opportunity cost is the reduced spending on education, transport, power supply or telecommunications.

A second example of opportunity cost is from within the healthcare budget. As shown in Table 1, resources have to be allocated between competing areas such as hospital services, medical equipment and public health services. So, if doctors and nurses were given a pay rise, the opportunity cost would be the reduced funding that would be available for other hospital services such as new up-to-date equipment for surgical work.

TIP

Part d does not ask for a definition of opportunity cost. It would be helpful for your explanation to show that you understand this concept.

TIP

Notice how the worked example answer draws upon the data.

2 Namibia's government faces a problem in deciding how to spend its income from tax revenue. The problem is that there is not enough funding to meet its spending. In 2023, it received $3.872m and it spent $4.281m. The government has to decide whether to prioritise the needs of consumers or producers, especially farmers who are seeking more support from the government as a result of a fall in their incomes due to low crop prices.

a	Define the 'basic economic problem'.	[2]
b	Explain **two** ways in which the basic economic problem applies when a government has to decide what to spend its tax revenue on.	[4]
c	Analyse, using a production possibility curve (PPC) diagram, how an economy is affected by having unemployed resources.	[6]
d	Discuss whether or not an increase in government spending might benefit consumers and farmers.	[8]

Total: [20]

Improve this answer

Here is a sample answer to part d:

The government's spending can affect consumers in various ways. The government will be popular if it increases spending on pensions, social services, unemployment benefits or education. Consumers will experience an immediate benefit. Consumers may also benefit if a government spent more on roads and railways. There could also be benefits for consumers when more money is spent on the army or a new parliament building. This spending may well trickle to consumers in terms of more jobs although this is difficult to prove.

Farmers are consumers as well as producers, so there are some benefits for them as referred to earlier. The principal way for them to benefit would be through higher prices for their produce. These prices might even be maximum prices.

> ### YOUR CHALLENGE
>
> See whether you can improve this answer. Before you write your answer, think about the points below:
>
> - The first paragraph demonstrates what follows – provided you have enough writing time.
> - The second paragraph demonstrates good understanding of the benefits to consumers. It covers a range of possibilities. Including a few more specific examples, from other information or case studies you have read, would provide more substance.
> - The last sentence refers to maximum prices. This is not correct, as maximum prices benefit consumers and not farmers. Farmers will benefit from minimum prices when these are set at a level that will provide them with a living income.
> - The main weakness in terms of content is that the answer is unbalanced. More content is needed on how increased government spending could affect farmers. For example, you could refer to the link between prices and farmer's incomes.
> - For this question, it is necessary to consider both sides of the argument based on what has been written. It should make clear whether increased government spending might benefit both consumers and farmers. Alternatively, it could be concluded that consumers are more likely to benefit than farmers or that farmers are more likely to benefit than consumers.

Section 2
The allocation of resources

> Chapter 5
The role of markets in allocating resources

LEARNING INTENTIONS

By the end of this chapter, you will be able to:
- define a market
- give examples of markets
- explain the roles of buyers and sellers.

KEY TERMS

consumers	firm	market	raw materials

Key skills activities

1 Link each example of a product market with the way it brings buyers and sellers into contact with each other.

Market
Fruit
Rare books
Second-hand bicycles
Soap powder
Trainers/sneakers

Way of bringing buyers and sellers into contact with each other
Auction
Local noticeboard
Market stall
Online
Supermarket

5 The role of markets in allocating resources

2 Find a six-letter economics term by using the first letter of each word that could apply in the following cases. One has been done for you.

Clue	Answer
Items that a hospital buys	
Items that a fruit shop may sell	
Items that a carpet shop may sell	
Items that a Japanese clothes shop may sell	Kimonos
Items that may be bought from a farm shop	
What buyers and sellers do	

Economics term: _ _ _ K_ _

TIP

Remember that households, firms and the government can be both buyers and sellers.

3 In every market, there are buyers and sellers. In the case of the five markets below, identify a possible name for the buyers and a name for the sellers. The first letter of the name for the buyers and the name for the sellers gives the internet domain name for a country in each case. The countries are given and should help you. The first one is also done for you.

a Market: computers. Internet domain name for: Sweden.

Buyers: shoppers. Sellers: electronics stores. Internet domain name: se

b Market: spectacles. Internet domain name for: Colombia.

c Market: hair cutting and styling. Internet domain name for: Switzerland.

d Market: flights from Asia to Europe. Internet domain name for: Panama.

e Market: handmade suits. Internet domain name for: Portugal.

Write your answers in your notebook.

SELF-ASSESSMENT

Do you feel confident that you could, for example, name three items that a school might buy and three types of arrangements that could bring the school in contact with the sellers of these items?

Chapter 5 practice questions

Circle the correct answer to each question.

1 Which is the largest market?

    A   The car market in Asia

    B   The car market in Beijing, capital of China

    C   The car market in China

    D   The global car market   [1]

2 What is the most likely reason a seller of tea will leave the market?

    A   A decrease in the number of other sellers of tea

    B   A decrease in the popularity of drinking coffee

    C   An increase in the amount buyers have to spend

    D   An increase in the number of days of bad weather in tea-growing areas   [1]

3 Which market is most likely to be smaller in 2050 than it is now?

    A   Education

    B   Healthcare

    C   Oil

    D   Tourism   [1]

Total: [3]

Chapter 6
Demand

LEARNING INTENTIONS

By the end of this chapter, you will be able to:
- define demand
- recognise the link between individual and market demand
- draw and interpret the demand diagram
- explain the causes of extensions and contractions in demand
- draw diagrams that illustrate movements along a demand curve
- analyse the causes of increases and decreases in demand
- draw diagrams that illustrate shifts of the demand curve.

KEY TERMS

ageing population   aggregation   birth rate   change in demand
complement   contraction in demand   decrease in demand
demand   extension in demand   increase in demand
inferior goods   normal goods   substitute

Key skills activities

1 Link each key term to its correct definition.

Term
Aggregation
Complement
Contraction in demand
Decrease in demand
Substitute

Definition
A fall in demand at any given price, causing the demand curve to shift to the left.
A fall in the quantity demanded caused by a rise in the price of the product.
A product that can be used in place of another.
A product that is used together with another product.
The addition of individual units to arrive at a total amount.

2   Products A, B, C, D, E and F have five consumers. Table 6.1 shows how many products each would demand at $8.

Table 6.1: Consumer demand for different products

	Consumer 1	Consumer 2	Consumer 3	Consumer 4	Consumer 5
Product A	6	9	4	3	2
Product B	3	5	2	2	4
Product C	40	21	19	6	11
Product D	4	2	7	8	10
Product E	10	11	10	11	16
Product F	2	4	3	1	1

a   Calculate the market demand for each of the six products.

b   Using all the market demand figures by adding, dividing, multiplying or subtracting them, show how a figure of 10 could be arrived at.

This is very tricky. You may want to work on this with a partner. To give you an example, if the figures were 10, 21, 41, 30, 25 and 15, a figure of 17 could be arrived at with the following calculations:

10 + 21 + 41 = 72

72 − 30 = 42

42 − 25 = 17

Write your answers in your notebook.

TIP

Remember, demand in economics does not mean simply to want something. To count as demand, people not only have to want a product, they also have to be able to buy the product.

3   Figure 6.1 shows different quantities demanded at different prices.

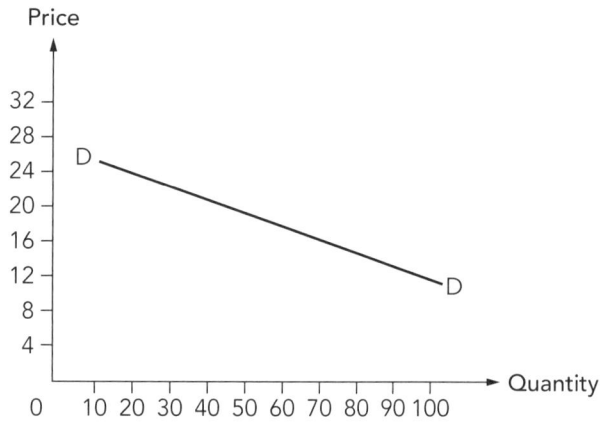

Figure 6.1: A demand curve

Using Figure 6.1, find:

a The quantity that will be demanded at a price of $20

b How much quantity demanded would extend if price falls from $20 to $16

c How much quantity demanded would contract if price rises from $20 to $24

Write your answers in your notebook.

> **SELF-ASSESSMENT**
>
> How confident did you feel completing Activity 3? Think about the points below. Then, using different figures, draw a demand curve diagram. Write three questions and explanations of the answers for another student.
>
> - Did you use a ruler to link the price and the quantity demanded in each case?
> - Did you calculate the change in quantity demanded in each case rather than just the new quantity demanded?

> **TIP**
>
> Remember that for most products, price and demand move in the opposite directions – they are inversely related.

4 In Figure 6.2, diagrams A–D relate to the market for gel pens.

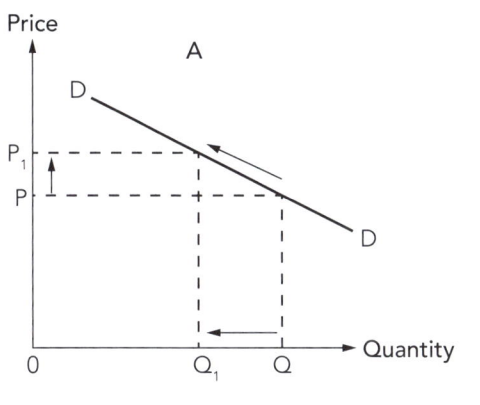
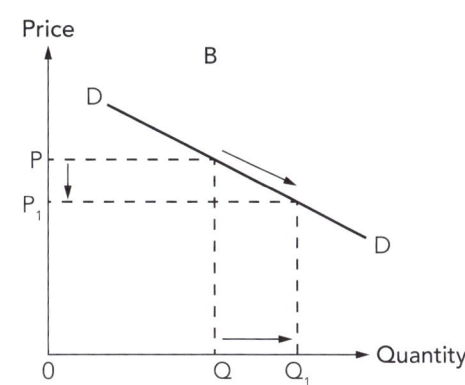
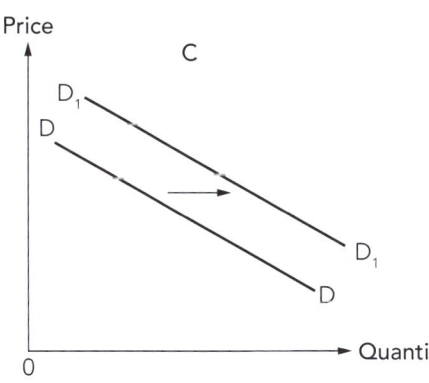
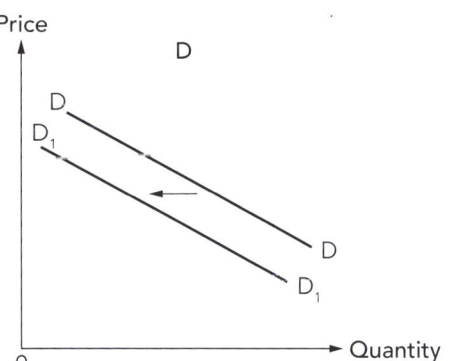

Figure 6.2: Market for gel pens

Explain which diagram in Figure 6.2 shows:

a   A fall in the price of paper

b   A fall in the price of gel pens

c   A fall in the price of ballpoint pens.

Write your answers in your notebook.

 5   Complete the crossword using the clues below. You can download the crossword grid (Worksheet 6.5) from GO.

Across

1   A fall in the quantity demanded of a product caused by a rise in price. (11)

3   What is measured on the horizontal axis of a demand curve. (8)

5   The direction demand moves along a demand curve due to a rise in price. (2)

7   The willingness and ability to buy a product. (6)

9   The name for a change in the position of a demand curve due to a change in an influence other than price. (5)

10   The name for the total demand for a product. (6)

13   The direction a demand curve moves when less is demanded at each and every price. (4)

15   A rise in demand resulting from a change in an influence other than a change in price. (8)

16   A movement along a demand curve resulting in a higher quantity demanded. (9)

Down

1   A line joining up different quantities demanded or supplied at different prices. (5)

2   The name for a schedule or curve which shows the demand of one person. (10)

4   The direction along a demand curve resulting from a fall in price. (4)

6   What is on the vertical axis of a demand diagram. (5)

8   A shift to the left of a demand curve. (8)

11   The direction of a change in a demand curve as a result of an increase in the price of a substitute. (5)

12   Portable shelters for people to sleep in sold by a camping firm. (5)

14   The speed at which a camping firm would want to respond to an increase in demand for one of its products. (4)

Chapter 6 practice questions

Circle the correct answer to each question.

1 Linen shirts are a substitute to cotton shirts. What effect will a fall in the price of linen shirts have on demand for cotton shirts?

   A A contraction in demand

   B A decrease in demand

   C An extension in demand

   D An increase in demand [1]

2 What is the most likely cause of a shift to the left of the demand curve for luxury soap?

   A A decrease in income

   B A decrease in the price of toothpaste

   C An increase in advertising expenditure on luxury soap

   D An increase in the price of luxury soap [1]

3 What may cause the demand for goats' milk to differ in different countries?

	Differences in income	Differences in price of cows' milk	Differences in population size	Differences in tastes
A	✓	✗	✗	✗
B	✓	✓	✗	✗
C	✓	✓	✓	✗
D	✓	✓	✓	✓

[1]

4 What does a demand schedule show?

   A The different prices that have been charged for a product over a particular time period

   B The different products a person intends to buy over a particular time period

   C The different quantities demanded of a product at different prices over a particular time period

   D The different quantities of a product people would like to buy over a particular time period [1]

5 Which combination of products is most likely to be substitutes?

   A   Peaches and cream

   B   Peaches and pears

   C   Pineapples and bread

   D   Pineapples and haircuts [1]

   Total: [5]

Chapter 7
Supply

> **LEARNING INTENTIONS**
>
> By the end of this chapter, you will be able to:
> - define supply
> - recognise the link between individual and market supply
> - explain the causes of extensions and contractions in supply
> - draw a diagram to illustrate a movement along a supply curve
> - analyse the causes of shifts in the supply curve
> - draw diagrams that illustrate shifts of a supply curve.

> **KEY TERMS**
>
> change in supply   contraction in supply
> decrease in supply   direct taxes   extension in supply
> improvements in technology   individual supply
> increase in supply   indirect taxes
> market supply   subsidy   tax   unit cost

Key skills activities

1 Link each key term to its correct definition.

Term
Change in supply
Increase in supply
Market supply
Subsidy
Supply

Definition
A payment by a government to encourage the production or consumption of a product.
A rise in supply at any given price, causing the supply curve to shift to the right.
Changes in supply conditions causing shifts in the supply curve.
Total supply of a product.
The willingness and ability to sell a product.

2 a In your notebook, write down one way in which each of the following pairs is similar. The first one has been done for you.

  i Demand curve and supply curve

  Both show different quantities at different prices of a product.

  ii Contraction in supply and contraction in demand

  iii Market demand and market supply

  iv Increase in demand and increase in supply

  v Vertical axis of a demand diagram and vertical axis of a supply diagram

b Write down one way in which each of the following pairs is different. The second one has been done for you.

  i Individual supply and market supply

  ii Production and supply

  Production is making a product, whereas supply is selling a product. Not all that is produced may be sold and, in a given time period, more may be sold than is produced if stocks are reduced.

  iii Demand and supply

  iv Decrease in supply and extension in supply

  v Extension in demand and extension in supply

SELF-ASSESSMENT

How confident did you feel completing Activity 2? Think about the points below. Then circle the number of smiley faces to show your level of confidence from 1 (need to revisit my understanding of price elasticity of supply (PES)) to 5 (feeling very confident).

- Are you clear on the similarities and differences between demand and supply?
- Are you aware why buyers and sellers respond in different ways to changes in price?
- What will you do to increase your understanding?

3 Table 7.1 shows the original quantity and a new quantity supplied over a range of prices.

Table 7.1: Original and new quantity supplied

Price ($)	Original quantity supplied	New quantity supplied
3	20	30
4	38	48
5	56	66
6	70	80
7	80	90

a Plot the two supply curves on a diagram.

b What effect would a rise in price from $6 to $7 have on supply?

c Explain whether the new supply curve shows a decrease or an increase in supply.

Write your answers in your notebook.

> **TIP**
>
> A diagram needs to be both accurate and clear. Do not make your diagrams too small. A quarter of a page is a useful size.

4 Link a cause of a change in supply with an appropriate product.

Cause of a change in supply
A fall in the cost of production due to advances in technology.
A fall in the cost of production due to cheaper raw materials.
A flood.
An increase in a government subsidy given to producers.
An increase in an indirect tax imposed on a product.
Discovery of new source.

Product
Furniture
Games console
Gold
High-sugar drink
Renewable energy
Tea

5 You have been appointed as an economic adviser to a firm making electric scooters.

Produce a presentation on what may cause the firm's supply to change in the future.

Chapter 7 practice questions

Circle the correct answer to each question.

1   What would cause a shift to the left of the supply curve for gold rings?

    A   A decrease in the price of complementary goods

    B   A decrease in the price of silver rings

    C   An increase in a government subsidy given to producers of gold rings

    D   An increase in the wages of workers producing gold rings [1]

2   A book publisher initially supplied 7000 books at a price of $40 per book.
    A month later, it supplied the same number of books at a price of $45 per book.
    What happened to its supply?

    A   It contracted

    B   It decreased

    C   It extended

    D   It increased [1]

3   What would cause a downward movement along a supply curve?

    A   A decrease in costs of production

    B   A decrease in price

    C   An increase in costs of production

    D   An increase in price [1]

4   What effect will an increase in a sales tax have on the supply of a product?

    A   A contraction in supply

    B   A decrease in supply

    C   An extension in supply

    D   An increase in supply [1]

5   What is a possible reason why the supply of a product falls when price decreases?

    A   Factors of production including labour reduce in quantity

    B   Firms switch to producing other products which have become more profitable

    C   Technological advances reduce costs of production

    D   The government reduces the subsidy given to firms [1]

Total: [5]

> Chapter 8
Price determination

> **LEARNING INTENTIONS**
>
> By the end of this chapter, you will be able to:
>
> - explain how the price mechanism answers the basic resource allocation questions
> - define market equilibrium
> - interpret equilibrium price and quantity in a market using demand and supply schedules
> - draw and interpret equilibrium price and quantity using demand and supply curves
> - define market disequilibrium
> - interpret disequilibrium prices and quantities in a market using demand and supply schedules
> - draw and interpret disequilibrium prices and quantities using demand and supply curves
> - explain shortages and surpluses.

> **KEY TERMS**
>
> | demand | market disequilibrium | market equilibrium |
> | --- | --- | --- |
> | price mechanism | shortage | supply | surplus |

Key skills activities

1 You are organising a fun event to raise money for a local charity. You have asked a local firm to sell bottled water at the event. The firm provides the supply schedule shown in Table 8.1, showing how many bottles it would be willing and able to sell over a range of prices.

Table 8.1: Supply schedule for bottled water

Price ($)	Quantity supplied
0.50	1
0.75	2
1.00	4
1.25	7
1.50	11
1.75	16
2.00	22
2.25	30

Note: you may change $ into your own currency here.

a   How many bottles of water would you be willing and able to buy at the different prices? From the information, draw up a demand schedule.

b   What is the equilibrium price?

Write your answers in your notebook.

TIP

Remember, equilibrium means 'balance' – and what is being balanced when there is an equilibrium price and quantity is demand and supply.

2   Figure 8.1 shows that price is initially $3.

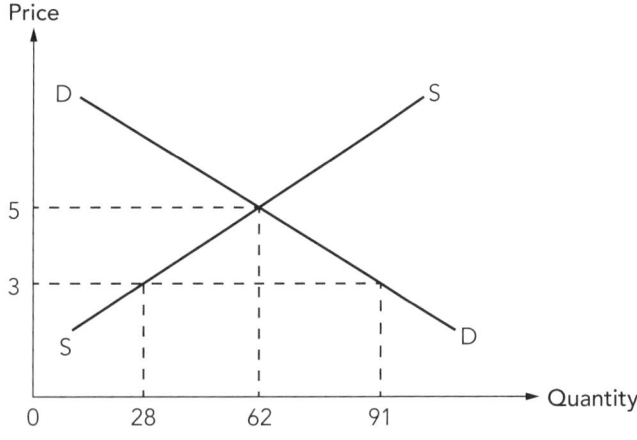

Figure 8.1: A demand and supply diagram

Using Figure 8.1, identify:

a   The initial shortage

b   By how much demand contracts when the price moves to the market equilibrium

c   By how much supply extends when the price moves to the market equilibrium.

Write your answers in a notebook.

8 Price determination

> **SELF-ASSESSMENT**
>
> How confident did you feel completing Activity 2? What might you do to build on your understanding of how markets move from disequilibrium to equilibrium?

 3   Complete the crossword using the clues below. You can download the crossword grid (Worksheet 8.3) from GO.

Across

1 A situation where demand and supply are not equal. (14)

5 What is measured on the horizontal axis of a demand and supply diagram. (8)

6 What is measured on the vertical axis of a demand and supply diagram. (5)

8 Where demand moves on a demand curve when price changes – .... the curve. (5)

9 Are price and demand inversely related? (3)

10 Excess demand. (8)

11 Total amount. (3)

13 Excess supply. (7)

17 The direction of the shift in the demand curve when there is an increase in demand. (5)

18 The name for an individual or a firm who sells a product. (6)

19 The direction of the shift in the supply curve when there is a decrease in supply. (4)

Down

1 The willingness and ability to buy a product. (6)

2 A situation where demand and supply are equal. (11)

3 People who purchase goods and services (6)

4 A list, for example, of the different quantities demanded at different prices. (8)

7 What supply will do as a result of a higher price. (4)

9 Are supply and price directly related? (3)

10 The willingness and ability to sell a product. (6)

12 An arrangement which brings buyers into contact with sellers. (6)

14 The amount of money that has to be given in payment for a good or service. (5)

15 A movement of a demand or supply curve to the left or the right of the original one. (5)

16 A total amount. (5)

Chapter 8 practice questions

Circle the correct answer to each question.

1 A market is operating with a disequilibrium price. What must this mean?

    A   Demand and supply are not equal

    B   Shortages do not exist

    C   The price mechanism is not working

    D   There is no opportunity cost involved   [1]

2 What must indicate that there is excess supply in a market?

    A   Price is below equilibrium

    B   Price is near equilibrium

    C   There is a shortage

    D   There is a surplus   [1]

3 Why is a long-run surplus likely to result in a decrease in production?

    A   Demand will exceed supply

    B   Demand will rise in the future

    C   Firms will not continue to produce if price rises

    D   Firms will not continue to produce more than they can sell   [1]

4 What would indicate that a market is not in equilibrium?

    A   The price is staying the same

    B   The quantity sold is equal to the quantity bought

    C   There are more buyers than sellers

    D   There is a waiting list for the product   [1]

5   The demand and supply schedules of a product are initially:

Price ($)	Quantity demanded	Quantity supplied
75	10	49
70	20	48
65	30	45
60	40	40
55	50	34
50	60	26

If demand increases by 50% at each price, what would be the new equilibrium price?

A $55

B $60

C $65

D $70   [1]

Total: [5]

Chapter 9
Price changes

LEARNING INTENTIONS

By the end of this chapter, you will be able to:

- analyse how changes in demand supply can cause price changes
- use demand and supply diagrams to illustrate how changes in demand and supply affect price
- analyse the consequences of price changes.

KEY TERMS

equilibrium price   equilibrium sales

Key skills activities

1 Complete each of the following sequences to show what happens next. The first one has been done for you.

   a   Demand increases → Price rises → Supply extends → Quantity traded (sales) rises

   b   Demand decreases → Price falls → .... → Quantity traded (sales) falls

   c   Supply decreases → .... → Demand contracts → Quantity traded (sales) falls

   d   Supply increases → .... → .... → ....

> **TIP**
>
> Remember, the *cause* of a change in price is a decrease or an increase in demand or supply. The *consequence* of a change in price is an extension or contraction in demand or supply.

2 Link each of the price changes that has occurred over time with its cause.

Price change(s)
Fall in the price of calculators
Fall in the price of laptops
Fluctuations in the price of cryptocurrencies
Rise in price of season ticket to watch a top-flight football team

Cause
Decrease in demand
Decrease and increase in demand
Increase in demand
Increase in supply

3 Figure 9.1 shows the market for bus travel.

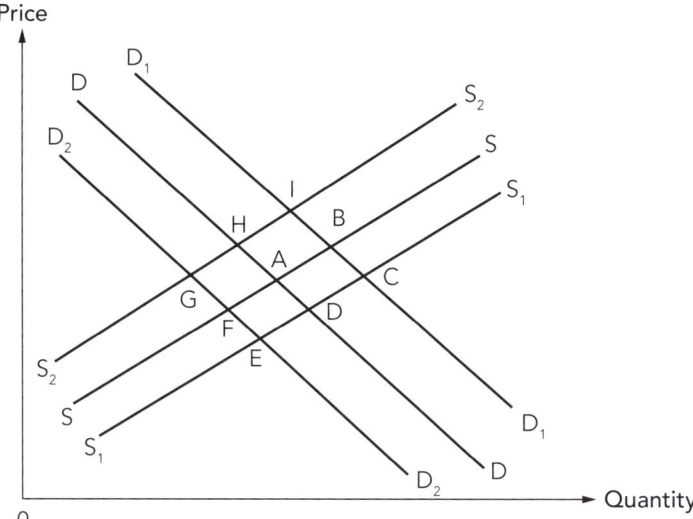

Figure 9.1: Market for bus travel

Using Figure 9.1, starting each time at the initial equilibrium of A, explain what will be the new equilibrium in each of the following cases:

a A fall in the price of train travel

b An increase in population

c An increase in the price of fuel that is used to power buses

d A government subsidy given to bus firms

e An increase in the punctuality of buses and the introduction of driverless buses.

Write your answers in your notebook.

SELF-ASSESSMENT

How confident did you feel completing Activity 3? Would you be able to explain your answers to another student? Think about the points below. Then circle the number of smiley faces to show your level of confidence from 1 (need to revisit my understanding of price changes) to 5 (feeling very confident).

- Do you know the difference between influences on demand and supply?
- Do you understand the difference in the direction demand and supply curves move when there are increases and when there are decreases?

4 All of the words in the box are related to price changes. See if you can find them in the wordsearch. You can download the wordsearch (Worksheet 9.4) from GO to complete it.

buyers	diagram	equilibrium	excess demand
excess supply	sellers	shortage	supply
	surplus	unequal	

Chapter 9 practice questions

Circle the correct answer to each question.

1 A contraction in supply is:

   A   A cause of a fall in price

   B   A cause of a rise in price

   C   A consequence of a fall in price

   D   A consequence of a rise in price [1]

2 What could cause the equilibrium quantity to increase but the equilibrium price to remain unchanged?

   A   Demand increased by more than supply

   B   Supply increased by more than demand

   C   The decrease in demand was matched by the increase in supply

   D   The increase in demand was matched by the increase in supply [1]

TIP

Drawing diagrams to show changes, like those in question 2, may help you to choose your answer option.

3 What may cause an increase in both the demand and supply of a product?

   A   Advances in technology that improve quality and reduce the cost of production

   B   Government subsidies given to producers that increase the incentive to increase output and lower price

   C   Removal of an indirect tax that lowers the cost of production and increases firms' profits

   D   Rise in incomes that increase consumers' willingness and ability to buy the product [1]

4 What is meant by 'a market clearing price'?

  A A disequilibrium price

  B A price below equilibrium

  C The price at which demand is driven down to its lowest level

  D The price at which demand is in balance with supply [1]

5 Which combination of changes includes a cause of a decrease in supply and a consequence of a decrease in supply?

  A A decrease in costs of production and a fall in price

  B A decrease in incomes and a decrease in demand

  C An increase in an indirect tax and a rise in price

  D An increase in population and a rise in price [1]

Total: [5]

> Chapter 10

Price elasticity of demand (PED)

LEARNING INTENTIONS

By the end of this chapter, you will be able to:

- define price elasticity of demand (PED)
- calculate price elasticity of demand
- interpret the significance of the PED value: perfectly inelastic, inelastic, unitary elastic, elastic, perfectly elastic
- draw and interpret demand curve diagrams to show PED
- analyse the main influences on whether demand is elastic or inelastic
- explain the relationship between PED and the amount spent by consumers and revenue raised by firms
- discuss the implications of PED for decision-making by consumers, workers, producers/firms and government.

KEY TERMS

elastic demand   inelastic demand   perfectly elastic demand

perfectly inelastic demand   price elasticity of demand (PED)

unitary elastic demand

Key skills activities

1 To find the name of a famous economist, you first need to undertake the following PED calculations. The first one has been done for you.

    a PED is unitary. If price falls by 19%, what would be the percentage change in quantity demanded?

        19%: $\frac{19\%}{-19\%}$ would give a PED of -1

    b If the quantity demanded contracts by 20% when price rises by 4%, what is the PED?

    c If the PED is -2 and demand extends by 22%, what is the percentage change in price?

d The PED is –0.8. If demand extends from 200 to 240, what must have been the percentage fall in price?

e Demand contracts from 2 000 to 1 200 as a result of a rise in price from $50 to $54. What is the PED?

f If the PED is –3 when demand contracts by 42%, what is the percentage change in price?

When you have found all the figures, convert them into letters with 1 being A, 2 being B, up to Z being 26. So, in this case, 19 converts to S, the 19th letter of the alphabet. Rearrange the letters to form the name of a famous economist (you may have to research the name of famous economists). You may wish to check the letters and work out the anagram of the famous economist with another student.

Famous economist: ....

> **TIP**
>
> When calculating and writing about PED, it is important to remember that PED is involved with percentage changes. Demand may contract by a small number, for example five, and price may rise by an even smaller amount, for example $1, but demand might still be inelastic. This is because PED examines relative changes. In this case, price may rise from $10 to $11 (10%) causing demand to contract from 200 to 195 (2.5%), the PED would be –0.25.

2 Figure 10.1 shows a demand diagram.

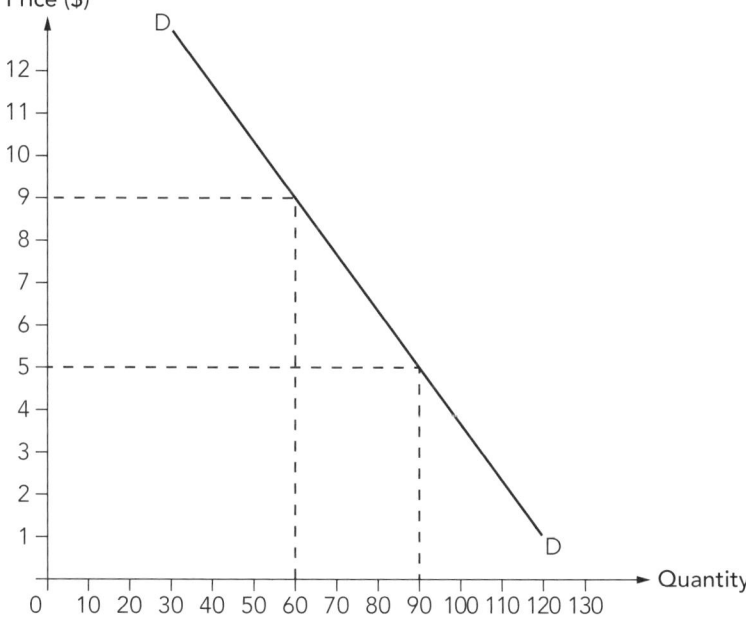

Figure 10.1: Demand diagram

Using Figure 10.1, write the answers to these questions in your notebook:

a   What is total amount spent by consumers when price is $5?

b   What is the total revenue earned by producers when price is $5?

c   What is the change in revenue if producers raise the price to $9?

d   What is the PED when price rises from $5 to $9?

e   Explain, whether in this case, you would recommend that producers should raise the price from $5 to $9.

If you have time, draw another demand diagram with different prices and quantities and write questions based on your figures. Swap your diagram and questions with another student.

3   Complete Table 10.1 to show the differences between elastic demand and inelastic demand.

Table 10.1: Differences between elastic demand and inelastic demand

	Elastic demand	Inelastic demand
Effect of a rise in price on revenue		Increase
Effect of a fall in price on revenue		
Availability of close substitutes	High	
Luxury or necessity		
Proportion of income spent		Low
Ability to postpone purchase	Yes	

SELF-ASSESSMENT

How confident did you feel completing Activity 3? Think about the points below.

- Do you understand the difference between the effect of a rise in price on demand and on revenue?

- Are you able to recognise the key differences between elastic demand and inelastic demand?

Would you be able to construct a table comparing perfectly inelastic demand and inelastic demand?

4 Complete each sequence below. Explain the reason for the word(s) you have chosen in each case. The first sequence has been done for you.

Perfectly elastic	Elastic	Unitary elastic	Inelastic	Inelastic - PED becomes more inelastic as you move from left to right and more elastic as you move from right to left.
Food	Vegetables	Onions	Red onions	
Drinks	Soft drinks	Fruit juice	Pineapple juice	
Calculate %ΔQD	Calculate %ΔP	Divide %ΔQD by %ΔP	PED	

5 The owner of the firm is considering raising the price of the product. Explain whether each of the following people would welcome such a rise. You may want to discuss your answers with another student.

- Consumer
- Owner of the firm
- Owner of a firm that produces a substitute good
- Government minister
- Worker.

Write your answers in your notebook.

Chapter 10 practice questions

Circle the correct answer to each question.

1 What happens to PED on a straight-line demand curve as price rises?

    A It becomes more elastic

    B It becomes more inelastic

    C It moves towards perfectly inelastic demand

    D It stays at unit price elasticity of demand   [1]

2 A firm lowers the price of its product and finds that its total revenue increases. What would this mean?

    A PED is greater than one

    B PED is less than one

    C PED is one

    D PED is zero   [1]

3   A fall in price results in an equal percentage fall in consumer expenditure
    on the product. What would this mean?

    A   PED is greater than one

    B   PED is infinity

    C   PED is less than one

    D   PED is one [1]

4   Which statement about price elasticity of demand is correct?

    A   Price elasticity of demand increases when the demand curve shifts to
        the left

    B   Price elasticity of demand is concerned with absolute and not percentage
        changes

    C   When demand is price elastic, a rise in price will reduce the quantity
        demanded but raise consumer expenditure on the product

    D   When demand is price inelastic, a rise in price will increase the quantity
        demanded but reduce total revenue from the sale of the product [1]

5   A government seeks to raise revenue from a tax on a product.
    Which value of PED would be most successful in raising tax revenue?

    A   −0.2

    B   −0.8

    C   −1.2

    D   −1.8 [1]

Total: [5]

> Chapter 11

Price elasticity of supply (PES)

LEARNING INTENTIONS

By the end of this chapter, you will be able to:

- define price elasticity of supply (PES)
- calculate price elasticity of supply (PES)
- draw and interpret demand curve diagrams to show different PES
- interpret the significance of the PES value: perfectly inelastic, inelastic, unitary elastic, elastic, perfectly elastic
- analyse the main influences on whether supply is elastic or inelastic.

KEY TERMS

elastic supply   inelastic supply   perfectly elastic supply
perfectly inelastic supply   price elasticity of supply (PES)
unitary elastic

1   Link each key term to its correct definition. An example has been done for you.

Term	Definition
Elastic supply	A measure of the responsiveness of the quantity supplied to a change in price.
Inelastic supply	When a change in price causes a complete change in quantity supplied.
Perfectly elastic supply	When a change in price causes an equal percentage change in the quantity supplied.
Perfectly inelastic supply	When a change in price has no effect on quantity supplied.
Price elasticity of supply	When the quantity supplied changes by a greater percentage than the percentage change in price.
Unitary elastic	When the quantity supplied changes by a smaller percentage than the percentage change in price

2   Table 11.1 shows the key influences on PES. Complete the table to show whether the influence on PES is 'high' or 'low'. Some examples have been done for you.

Table 11.1: Influences on PES

	Elastic supply	Inelastic supply
Ability to store	High	Low
Availability of spare resources		
Cost of altering supply	Low	
Production time		
Use of existing resources		

> **TIP**
>
> In explaining the difference between economic goods and free goods, it is often useful to give examples.

3   The following are all incorrect statements about PES. Explain in each case of why the statement is incorrect.

   a   The formula for PES is change in supply divided by change in price.

   b   Elastic supply is when supply changes by more than demand.

   c   Price is initially $20 and supply is 500. If a rise in price to $30 results in a rise in supply to 600, PES is 2.5.

   Write your answers in your notebook.

> **TIP**
>
> Sometimes economists simply refer to 'elasticity of supply'. While there are different forms of elasticity of demand, there is only **one** form of elasticity of supply.

SELF-ASSESSMENT

How confident did you feel completing Activity 3? Think about the points below. Then try explaining to another student why the statements in the question are incorrect.

- In answering 3a, did you have to check what the formula is? Would you find it useful to include it on a revision card?

- In answering 3b, did you recognise that there are two reasons why the statement is incorrect? If not, check the definition of elastic supply and highlight key words.

- To answer 3c, you needed to do the calculation. You are likely to need to calculate PES several times before you become fully confident.

4   Using the appropriate formula, in each case, calculate PES. You may find it helpful to use a calculator.

   a   The quantity supplied falls by 6% when price falls by 30%.

   b   A 10% rise in price results in supply extending from 40 to 60.

   c   A rise in price from $80 to $90 cause supply to extend from 240 to 360.

   Write your answers in your notebook. Include your workings.

> **TIP**
>
> Did you notice that in answering 4a you had to do **one** calculation, in 4b **two** calculations and in 4c **three** calculations?

5 Table 11.2 shows categories of PES. Complete the table. An example has been done for you.

Table 11.2: Categories of PES

Categories of PES	PES figure	Description of supply curve diagram
Elastic supply		
Inelastic supply		
Perfectly elastic supply		
Perfectly inelastic supply	0	Vertical line
Unitary supply		

6 You are employed as an economist by a chocolate manufacturer. The owners ask you to produce a report giving advice about the future strategy of the firm. The owners do not have a background in economics. In your report:

    a Write an explanation of what is meant by PES for the firm's owners.

    b You have estimated that the PES of the firm's main chocolate bar is 0.6. Explain what this means.

    c You advise that the firm should try to make the supply elastic. Analyse the advantages to a firm of having a PES greater than one.

> **TIP**
>
> Economics includes lots of technical terms. Explaining these to someone who has not studied economics is one of the best ways of testing your understanding.

7 Complete the sudoku. You can download the sudoku grid from GO (Worksheet 11.7). Each row, column and square should be filled out with the numbers 1 to 9, not repeating any numbers within a row, column or square. Answering questions a–e will provide you with five figures to fill in.

    a If the PES is 0.8 and supply rises by 2.4%, what is the percentage change in price?

    b If price falls by 40% and supply falls by 200%, what is the PES?

    c Price rises from $8 to $10 and supply extends from 200 to 300. What is the PES?

    d If supply changes by 18% when price changes by 6%, what is the PES?

    e How many categories of PES are there?

Chapter 11 practice questions

Circle the correct answer to each question.

1 Why is the supply of aeroplanes inelastic in the short run?

    A Air travel is a luxury

    B It takes a long time to build a plane

    C The cost of storing planes is low

    D There are no substitutes to planes   [1]

2 Which value of price elasticity of supply would benefit consumers the most?

   A   0

   B   1

   C   2

   D   3 [1]

3 Which product is likely to have the most elastic supply?

   A   Houses

   B   Rice

   C   Soap

   D   Washing machines [1]

4 Supply of a product is perfectly inelastic. What will be the description of its supply curve?

   A   Horizontal

   B   Shallow, upward sloping

   C   Steep, upward sloping

   D   Vertical [1]

5 It can take up to eight years for rubber trees to reach maturity. What is the price elasticity of rubber likely to be?

   A   Elastic

   B   Inelastic

   C   Perfectly elastic

   D   Perfectly inelastic [1]

Total: [5]

> Chapter 12
Market economic system

LEARNING INTENTIONS

By the end of this chapter, you will be able to:

- define a market economic system
- discuss the arguments for and against the market economic system.

KEY TERMS

capital-intensive   directives   economic system   free rider

labour-intensive   market economic system   market failure

planned economic system   price mechanism   privatisation

public sector   state-owned enterprises (SOEs)

Key skills activities

1 Figure 12.1 shows market signals that would cause the price to fall, rise or remain unchanged.

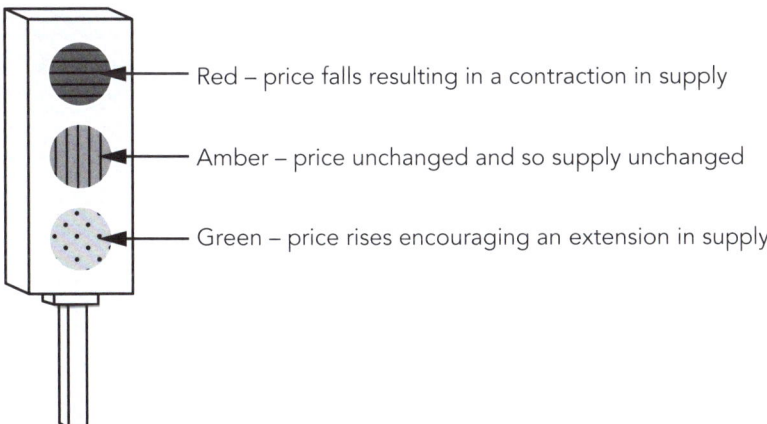

Figure 12.1: Market signals

Using Figure 12.1, decide which colour signal the price mechanism would be likely to send to producers of chocolate in each of the following situations:

a   A rise in the price of biscuits

b   A health report warning of the risks of eating too much chocolate

c   An increase in income

d   A switch from drinking orange juice to drinking pineapple juice

e   An increase in the popularity of ice cream.

Write your answers in your notebook. In each case, explain why you have chosen the colour.

 2 All the words in the box are related to the market economic system. See if you can find them in the wordsearch. You can download the wordsearch from GO to complete it (Worksheet 12.2).

choice	competition	efficient	enterprise
incentive	market forces	price	mechanism
	price signal	profit	quality

3 Either independently or in a pair, write a short report in your notebook identifying the features of a market economic system that are present in your country.

SELF-ASSESSMENT

How confident did you feel completing Activity 3? Think about the points below. Then see if you could produce a revision card on the main features of a market economic system.

- Do you understand how a market economic system allocates resources?
- Has the role of market forces changed in your country in recent years?

TIP

One way to remember the key nature of a market economic system is to realise the connection between 'market' in the term and 'market forces'.

 4 Download the mind map from GO (Worksheet 12.4) and complete it to give a summary of the market economic system.

Chapter 12 practice questions

Circle the correct answer to each question.

1   What is likely to be achieved by a market economic system?

   A   Absence of poverty

   B   Choice

   C   Equal distribution of income

   D   Full employment   [1]

12 Market economic system

2 How are prices determined in a market economic system?

    A Demand and supply

    B Government decisions

    C Public sector directives

    D Trade union's bargaining power [1]

3 What may cause prices to be low in a market economic system?

    A Competition

    B Government regulation

    C High incomes

    D Low supply [1]

4 What signals to producers in a market economic system that consumers have changed their demand?

    A The distribution of income

    B The existence of market power

    C The number of firms in the economy

    D The price mechanism [1]

5 What encourages private sector firms to produce what consumers demand?

    A The chance to earn a high profit

    B The chance to experience high unit cost of production

    C The desire to attract new firms into the industry

    D The desire to keep revenues as low as possible [1]

Total: [5]

Chapter 13
Market failure

> **LEARNING INTENTIONS**
>
> By the end of this chapter, you will be able to:
>
> - define market failure
> - explain key terms associated with market failure: public goods, merit goods, demerit goods, private benefits, external benefits, social benefits, private costs, external costs, social costs, monopoly
> - explain the causes of market failure relating to public goods, merit goods, demerit goods, external costs, external benefits and abuse of monopoly power
> - analyse the consequences of market failure.

> **KEY TERMS**
>
> demerit goods   external benefits   external costs
> information failure   merit goods   monopoly   price fixing
> private costs   private good   public good   social benefits
> social costs   socially optimum output   third parties

Key skills activities

1 Students often confuse merit goods and public goods. Complete Table 13.1, which compares the two.

Table 13.1: Merit good and public good

Feature	Merit good	Public good
Production without government intervention	Under-produced	
Excludable	Yes	
Rival		No
Private good		No
Example	Healthcare	

13 Market failure

 2 Complete the crossword using the clues below. You can download the crossword grid from GO (Worksheet 13.2).

Across

1. Not buying enough to achieve the socially optimum output. (5-11)
6. The term for costs imposed on third parties. (8)
7. An adverse (negative) effect of consuming or producing a product. (4)
8. A characteristic of a public good. (5)
9. A word that could be used to describe a party involved in a market transaction who is either the buyer or seller. (5)
10. The opposite of a public good. (7)
11. One item. (4)
13. A good or service that has to be provided by the government. (6)
14. An occupation that provides a merit good. (6)
15. A good or service that is more harmful than consumers may realise. (7)
17. To possess an item. (3)
18. A word that could be used to describe a party involved in a market transaction who is either the buyer or seller. (6)
19. A word to describe costs which include all the private and external costs. (4)
20. A person who is affected by external costs and external benefits. (5, 5)

Down

1. Making less of a product than the amount which would benefit society the most. (5-10)
2. The type of benefit which is social benefit minus private benefit. (8)
3. Buying more of a product than is beneficial for society. (5-11)
4. The forces of demand and supply resulting in an inefficient allocation of resources. (6, 7)
5. An occupation that provides a merit good. (7)
12. A word to describe total benefit. (6)
16. Free .... – someone who enjoys the benefits of a good or service without paying for it. (5)

TIP

In deciding whether a product is a public good or a private good, base your decision on whether it is produced or provided by the government, not on whether the government has to provide it. Think about whether market forces could provide the incentive for private sector firms to produce it.

> SELF-ASSESSMENT
>
> How confident did you feel completing Activity 2? Think about the points below.
>
> - Do you know the key definitions linked to market failure?
>
> - Do you understand the key difference between a merit good and a public good?
>
> Try explaining the difference between a merit good and a public good to someone in your family or a friend (who is not in your economics class). If you can make the difference clear to a non-economist, it should mean that you have really understood it!

3   External benefits and external costs both affect third parties. However, they have a number of differences. Complete Table 13.2, which compares the two.

Table 13.2: External benefits and external costs

	External benefits	External costs
Exist when:	Social benefits exceed social costs	
Effect on third parties	Beneficial	
Results in:		Over-consumption
Example of an activity that causes:	Taking a bus rather than driving a car	

4   The sentences below refer to why market failure may occur in connection with several products. Either individually or in a pair, decide which product in the box matches with each sentence and identify the nature of the market failure. In the case of the product you have not matched, write a sentence about why market failure may occur in its case. Part d has been done for you.

> Barcelona replica football shirts   cigarettes   fruit
>
> sea defences   steel   vaccinations

   a   Many people do not fully appreciate the full benefit they may gain from consuming the product.

   b   People consuming this product can help others.

   c   People who are not willing to pay cannot be excluded from consuming this product.

   d   Some people do not fully understand the health risks of consuming this product. *Cigarettes; demerit good*

   e   The producer of this product can charge high prices, as it is the only firm selling it.

   Write your answers in your notebook.

Chapter 13 practice questions

Circle the correct answer to each question.

1 Street lighting is not provided by market forces as it is not possible to charge directly for it. What type of good is street lighting?

   A   A demerit good

   B   A merit good

   C   A private good

   D   A public good [1]

2 What are the usual features associated with a merit good?

   A   External benefits and information failure

   B   External cost and free riders

   C   Private benefits and mobile resources

   D   Private costs and price fixing [1]

3 Why may a monopoly be able to charge a high price?

   A   Elastic demand for the product

   B   High number of competitors

   C   Lack of choice of suppliers

   D   Over-production of the product [1]

4 What is **not** a cause of market failure?

   A   Demand exceeding supply in the short run

   B   Existence of external benefits causing the product to be under-consumed

   C   Inability to prevent non-payers from consuming the product

   D   Lack of information causing producers to make inefficient choices [1]

5 Why are demerit goods overproduced?

   A   They are provided free

   B   They are overconsumed

   C   They have external benefits

   D   They have private costs [1]

Total: [5]

> Chapter 14
Mixed economic system

LEARNING INTENTIONS

By the end of this chapter, you will be able to:

- define a mixed economic system and discuss its advantages and disadvantages
- define a maximum price, draw and interpret a diagram showing a maximum price and analyse its advantages and disadvantages
- define a minimum price, draw and interpret a diagram showing a minimum price and analyse its advantages and disadvantages
- define indirect taxation, draw and interpret a diagram showing the effect of an indirect tax and analyse its advantages and disadvantages
- define a subsidy and draw and interpret a diagram showing the effect of a subsidy
- define regulation and analyse its advantages and disadvantages
- define privatisation and analyse its advantages and disadvantages
- define nationalisation and analyse its advantages and disadvantages
- define direct provision of goods and services and analyse its advantages and disadvantages
- define quotas and analyse their advantages and disadvantages.

KEY TERMS

lottery   mixed economic system   national champions
nationalisation (nationalise)   natural monopoly
public corporation   quotas   rationing   strategic industries

Key skills activities

1. Place the 15 words and phrases in the word cloud into five groups of three connected words/phrases and state how they are connected. Some words/phrases may fit into more than one group. However, there is only one solution that will give five groups of connected words/phrases. Complete the grid on the next page. One group has been done for you.

14 Mixed economic system

Decrease price	Goods and services tax (GST)
Increase government spending	Minimum price	Raise revenue
Excess supply	Increase competition	Indirect taxation
Price above equilibrium	Subsidy	Excise duty
Increase efficiency	Maximum price	Quota
Value added tax (VAT)		

Word group			Connection
Increase competition	Increase efficiency	Raise revenue	Reasons to privatise an industry

2 Complete the following sentences using the words in the box.

| beneficial | external | failure | free | private |
| prices | public | subsidy | tax | third |

a A merit good has both higher .... benefits than consumers realise and .... effects on .... parties.

b Market forces will not encourage private sector firms to produce .... goods, as those wanting the products can act as .... riders.

c Social costs minus private costs equals .... costs.

d To encourage the consumption of a merit good, a government may provide a .... to producers. In contrast, to discourage the consumption of a demerit good, it may place a .... on the product.

e   Information .... can result in consumers paying ....
    that are too high.

> **SELF-ASSESSMENT**
>
> How confident did you feel completing Activity 2? Think about the points below. Then produce a revision card based on answering the points.
>
> - Do you know the difference between a market economic system and a mixed economic system?
>
> - Do you understand how a government may try to influence the products people may consume?

 3 Complete the crossword using the clues below. You can download the crossword grid from GO (Worksheet 14.3).

Across

4   A charge by a government on the sale of products. (8, 8)

6   The direction in demand for products that cause external costs that a government would like to see. (4)

7   Laws and rules to influence economic activity. (10)

8   The direction in demand for products that cause external benefits that a government would like to see. (2)

13 To take ownership of industries into public ownership. (15)

14 The difference between demand and supply when price is not in equilibrium. (3)

15 Limits on the production or consumption of a product. (6)

16 Payments by a government to encourage the consumption or production of a product. (9)

18 Goods and services that are non-rival and non-excludable. (6)

19 The name for a price that producers cannot charge below. (7)

20 The name for total costs or benefits. (6)
21 Where a maximum price is set in comparison to the equilibrium price. (5)

Down

1 An arrangement for allocating resources that involves both the private and public sectors. (5, 8, 6)
2 A type of good or service that has more harmful effects on consumers than they realise. (7)
3 A government measure to stop the consumption or production of a good or service. (3)
5 Provide people with facts. (6)
9 The sale of a nationalised industry to the private sector. (13)
10 What a market will do if there are external benefits and external costs. (4)
11 A charge, below the equilibrium, for a product set by a government. (7, 5)
12 A tax on income or wealth. (6)
17 Poor-quality housing which can result from an uneven distribution of income. (5)

4 Produce a poster showing three ways to encourage the consumption of a merit good.

> **TIP**
>
> Be careful to avoid confusing a maximum price and a minimum price. You may find it helpful to draw diagrams to show both a maximum price and a minimum price on a revision card.

Chapter 14 practice questions

Circle the correct answer to each question.

1 Which type of good would a government not provide?

  A Demerit good

  B Merit good

  C Private good

  D Public good [1]

2 Why might a government set a maximum price?

  A To help people on low incomes

  B To help producers

  C To raise price

  D To raise tax revenue [1]

3 What evidence suggests that most economies operate a mixed economic system?

  A The existence of market failure

  B The existence of merit goods

    C   There are both renewable resources and non-renewable resources

    D   There is both a private sector and a public sector [1]

4 Which policy measure is a government likely to use to correct the market failure connected with a demerit good?

    A   Deregulation

    B   Privatisation

    C   Regulation

    D   Subsidy [1]

5 An indirect tax is charged on a product whose production creates pollution. What effect is this likely to have?

    A   It can turn external costs into external benefits

    B   It can turn external costs into private costs

    C   It can turn social benefits into private benefits

    D   It can turn social costs into social benefits [1]

Total: [5]

Section 2 practice questions

1 Read the source material carefully before answering all parts of the question.

China fact file	2023
Population	1.426bn
GDP per head	$12 720
Cars per '000 population	238

Globally, more than half of all electric vehicles (EVs) in use are in China. In 2022, new EV sales were around 8m, an increase of 82% on the previous year. Figure 1 shows total car sales from 2013 to 2023.

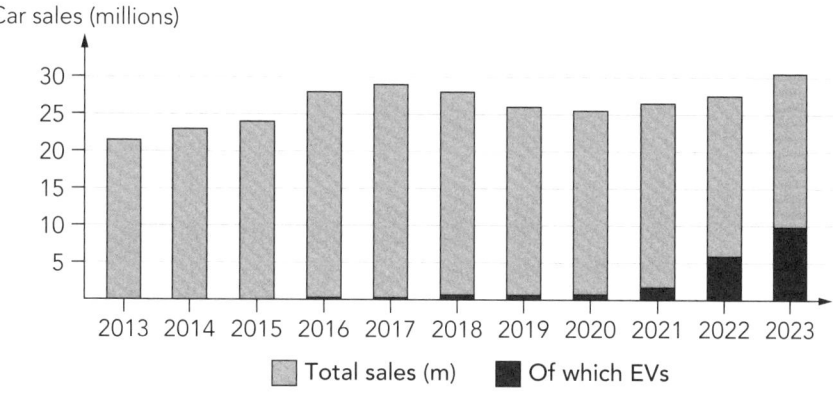

Figure 1: Total automobile sales in China, 2013–2023

The Chinese market is competitive in terms of price and choice. In 2022, over 100 new EV models were launched by Chinese car makers. The market share of Chinese brands in the domestic market increased to 56%. It was significant that most foreign brands, Japanese ones especially, seemed content to retain their range of models.

Chinese manufacturers exported 35% of their total production. These companies and others are keen to increase export sales, especially at times when surplus stock has accumulated due to weaker demand in the domestic market. It has been estimated that the price elasticity of demand for EVs in export markets is –0.8; in the domestic market, the price elasticity of demand is estimated to be –1.8.

Increased EV use is controversial. Not all would agree that the external benefits are greater than the external costs. This view stems from the argument that the manufacture of EVs requires the depletion of non-renewable resources and the use of fossil fuels. These costs are viewed as being greater than the benefits from their use compared to petrol and diesel vehicles. Nevertheless, many governments are aiming for a complete switch to EVs in the not too distant future.

Refer to the information in the source material in your answers.

a   Calculate the market share of EVs in the automobile market in China in 2023. [2]

b   Identify two reasons why the demand for EVs in China has increased since 2016. [2]

c   Explain how the equilibrium market price for EVs in China is determined. [2]

d   Draw a diagram to show how a surplus of vehicles affects the equilibrium of the EV market in China. [4]

e   Analyse why a Chinese EV producer is considering an increase in the prices of its auto exports but leaving prices unchanged in the domestic market. [4]

f   Discuss whether or not the external costs of EV production and use in China exceed the external benefits. [6]

Total: [20]

Improve this answer

Here is a sample answer to part e:

The price elasticity of demand (PED) is a measure of how the quantity demanded changes as a result of a change in the price of the product. This information can be used to see if the Chinese electric vehicle (EV) producer is right to increase export prices while keeping prices unchanged in the home market.

The main point to note is that the PED is inelastic for export EVs yet price elastic for EVs sold in the Chinese market. This shows that the domestic market for EVs is more competitive and that an increase in price will lead to lower sales and revenue for the producer. An increase in price for export EVs will also result in fewer sales but relatively less compared to the domestic market. The lower PED estimate seems to indicate that Chinese EVs are better value and quality compared to EVs manufactured elsewhere.

YOUR CHALLENGE

See whether you can improve this answer. Before you write your answer, think about the points below:

- The sample answer has a few valid points but contains significant errors in the interpretation of the data. The first paragraph could be omitted, as it represents the wording of the question, although there is a definition of PED in the first sentence.
- The first two sentences of the second paragraph are good, drawing on the difference between the two pieces of data. What follows is incorrect. This is because the formula for PED has been misremembered: the percentage change in quantity demanded has been used as the numerator and not the denominator. The last sentence about the nature of Chinese exports is OK, although it is not supported by the evidence.

TIP

Elasticity formulas are important. Do make sure to get them the right way round, otherwise your answer will be meaningless.

2 Read the source material carefully before answering all parts of the question.

Mauritius fact file	2023
Population	1.3 m
GDP per head	$8 892 (2022)
Unemployment rate	6.5%

Mauritius is an island in the Indian Ocean. It is well known for its beaches, lagoons and coral reefs that attract many international tourists. In 2019, almost 19% of its GDP was from spending by 1.4m international visitors. Most were from France, Germany and the UK. The island's other activities are sugar cane cultivation, textiles and clothing and financial services.

Table 1 shows tourism in Mauritius was hit hard in early 2020 by the COVID-19 pandemic.

Table 1: Actual and forecast tourist arrivals in Mauritius, 2019–2023

	2019	2020	2021	2022	2023
Tourist arrivals (m)	1.38	0.31	0.18	1.00	1.30
Forecast tourist arrivals (2018)	1.40	1.42	1.45	1.50	1.58

Travel restrictions, lockdowns and health fears resulted in an unprecedented fall in the number of visits by international tourists. Figure 2 shows that the unemployment rate increased as hotels, restaurants and tourist attractions had no alternative other than to lay off staff.

> **TIP**
>
> Look carefully at the data in Table 1. The bottom row is forecast data made in 2018 before the COVID-19 pandemic.

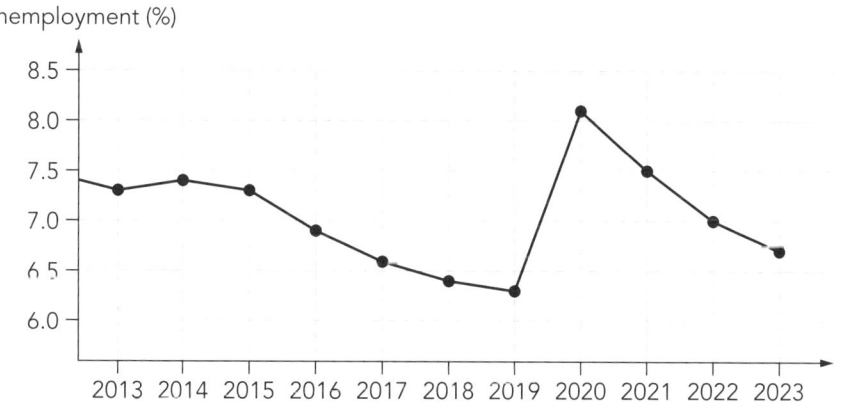

Figure 2: Unemployment rate in Mauritius, 2013–2023

COVID-19 caused particular difficulties for the government which in 2018 had stated that it planned to increase annual tourist numbers to 1.6m by 2024. This plan was to create over 40 000 new jobs, in particular to combat the growing problem of youth unemployment.

Not all of Mauritius's residents support this plan. They argue that it is not sustainable and point to increased pollution, soil erosion and habitat loss due to the increasing number of international tourists.

Refer to the information in the source material in your answers.

a   Calculate the difference between the forecast and the actual numbers of international tourists in 2020. [2]

b   Identify two reasons for the difference in the forecast and the actual numbers of international tourists in 2020. [2]

c   Explain one reason for the growth in international tourist arrivals in Mauritius in 2022 and 2023. [2]

d   Explain two benefits of increased international tourism for the economy of Mauritius. [4]

e   Analyse the relationship between the change in international tourist arrivals and the change in the unemployment rate from 2019. [4]

f   Discuss whether or not the government of Mauritius should keep to its plan to increase international tourist arrivals to 1.6m by 2024. [6]

Total: [20]

WORKED EXAMPLE FOR PART D

Employment. An increase in international tourists will create more jobs in hotels, restaurants and tourist attractions. Spending by those newly employed will create further jobs in the economy.

Foreign exchange. An increase in the number of international visitors will increase the foreign exchange receipts that are earned in the economy. These earnings are a form of export.

TIP

For part e, you will need to compare the data in Table 1 with data in Figure 2.

TIP

This question is best answered as in the worked example, where a relevant reason is stated followed by an explanation. Two sentences are likely to be all that's required to cover each benefit.

3   Widely grown in Southeast Asia, Malaysia is the largest producer of durians, a delicious fruit with a sweet flavour. Recent weather conditions have led to an abundant early harvest. Consumers have been slow to buy the fruit despite it being offered at $10 per kilogram, a 30% reduction on the usual market price. Growers are concerned that the fruit is perishing on trees, despite its discounted price.

a   Define 'price elasticity of supply'. [2]

b   Explain two reasons why the supply of fruit is usually price inelastic. [4]

c   Analyse how an increase in supply of fruit affects its market price. [6]

d   Discuss whether or not the market system can return the market price for durians to its usual price of $13 per kilogram. [8]

Total: [20]

Section 2 practice questions

WORKED EXAMPLE FOR PART C

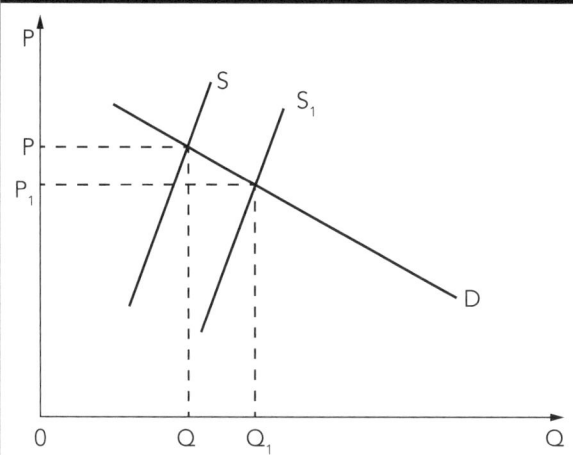

The market price is determined where the quantity demanded is equal to the quantity supplied. This is known as the equilibrium position. It is shown on the diagram where the price is P and the quantity is Q.

An increase in the supply of fruit can be caused by a good harvest. On the diagram, this situation is represented by a shift to the right of the supply curve from S to S1. The result is a fall in the market price from P to P1 and an increase in the quantity traded from Q to Q1. The extent of the changes in P and Q depends on the size of the shift of S to S1.

4 Poland's economy is a European success story. It has been transformed from a planned economy to a mixed economy over a 30-year period from the early 1990s. The economy now has the highest rate of GDP growth in the European Union (EU) and increasing living standards for its people. Its success can be attributed to being able to attract new private enterprises from elsewhere in Europe, the USA and Southeast Asia.

  a Define 'mixed economy'. [2]

  b Explain two ways in which an economy moves from being a planned to a mixed economy. [4]

  c Analyse how a maximum price can be applied in a mixed economy. [6]

  d Discuss whether or not private sector firms are always preferable to state-owned enterprises in a mixed economy. [8]

  Total: [20]

Improve this answer

Here is a sample answer to part c:

A maximum price is a type of price control imposed by a government in a mixed economy. It is usually placed on food items or electricity, the prices of which affect low-income people more than others. The maximum price is operating outside the scope of the free market system.

As the diagram shows, the maximum price is below the market equilibrium price of P.

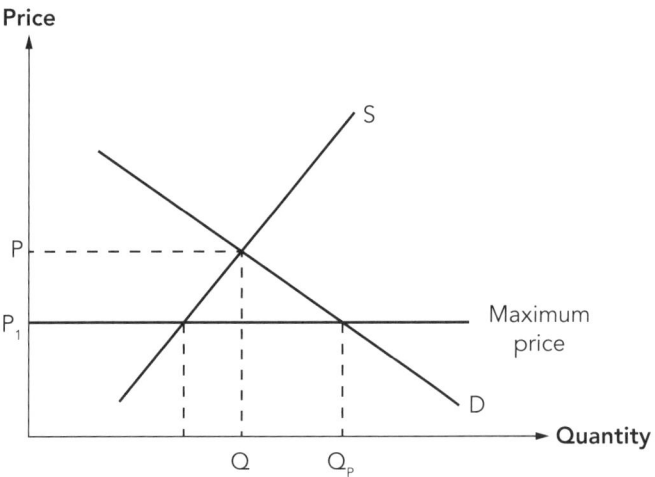

The diagram shows that with a maximum price of P1, the quantity demanded is QD and the quantity supplied QS. The problem is that it means more is demanded by consumers than is supplied by producers at this maximum price.

> ### YOUR CHALLENGE
>
> See whether you can improve this answer. Before you write your answer, think about the points below:
>
> - The example answer covers the basic aspects of maximum prices, but in terms of analysis, more could be added, particularly in the second paragraph which is too short. Better use could be made of the diagram, for example, the extent of shortage could be indicated. It could also be explained that some consumers will be disappointed as they are unable to buy the quantity they want. A brief reference to informal markets and rationing could conclude the answer.
> - The diagram is not quite complete. QS is left off the horizontal axis. A '0' (zero) should be inserted at the origin.
> - The sample answer is short – you would generally allow around 15 minutes' writing time for this six-mark question.

> Section 3
Microeconomic decision-makers

> Chapter 15

Money and banking

LEARNING INTENTIONS

By the end of this chapter, you will be able to:

- explain the forms, functions and characteristics of money
- analyse the role and importance of central banks and commercial banks.

KEY TERMS

central bank   commercial bank   interest
liquidity   money

Key skills activities

1. Link each function of money to its correct description.

Function of money
Medium of exchange
Standard for deferred payment
Store of value
Unit of account

Description
A way of comparing the value of different items.
Can be used to save for the future.
Enables households, firms and the government to borrow.
Used to buy and sell goods and services.

2. Design a questionnaire for other students, asking them to list eight things that will influence their choice of commercial bank in the future. For example, are they likely to be influenced by advertising on social media? Rank the responses you receive. Then, in your notebook, write a summary of what you found. Were the main influences the same as your own?

3. You are in charge of a commercial bank's lending policy. Decide which of the four firms, A–D, you would give a loan to and write an explanation of your choice.

   - Firm A: An established firm that owns six large coal mines in four countries. It made $1m profit last year. The firm wants a loan of $3m to open a coal mine in Australia.

TIP

Be careful to avoid confusing the functions and characteristics of money. Remember, there are four functions of money.

- Firm B: A hotel chain that has borrowed from the bank before and repaid on time. Last year, it made a loss of $0.2m. It wants a loan of $50 000 to repay a past loan which was given by another commercial bank.

- Firm C: A TV company that made a profit of $50 000 last year. It wants to borrow $0.5m to develop new programmes to stop the decline in its viewing figures and advertising revenue.

- Firm D: A new firm producing wind turbines with future orders of $4.5m over the next five years. It has estimated costs of $3m over the same period. It wants a loan of $0.6m to cover the difference between when it will receive its revenue from sales and when it will have to pay its costs.

Write your answers in your notebook.

4 The functions of a central bank can affect bank customers (consumers) bank employees (workers), commercial banks (firms) and government. Complete Table 15.1 by identifying a group that will be directly affected by a central bank function. Explain how this function may affect your chosen group. The first one has been done for you.

Table 15.1: How the functions of a central bank may affect different groups

Central bank function	Group	Explanation
Controls the banking system	Bank employees	Regulating commercial banks to ensure they follow sound practices may increase the job security of bank employees.
Implements monetary policy		
Issues bank notes		
Lender of last resort		

SELF-ASSESSMENT

How confident did you feel completing Activity 4? Think about the points below. Then see if you can produce a leaflet comparing the roles of a commercial bank and a central bank.

- Do you know the difference between a central bank and a commercial bank?

- Do you understand how central banks and commercial banks may affect different groups in the economy?

Chapter 15 practice questions

Circle the correct answer to each question.

1 Which of the following is a function of money?

   A   To enable people to borrow

   B   To encourage barter

   C   To help people become self-sufficient

   D   To reduce household debt [1]

2 Who holds accounts at the central bank?

   A   Commercial banks

   B   Households

   C   Manufacturing firms

   D   Workers [1]

3 Which function does the central bank carry out for the government?

   A   Imposes taxes

   B   Lends to households

   C   Manages the national debt

   D   Provides insurance for firms [1]

4 What is money held in a current (sight, demand deposit) account mainly used for?

   A   Medium of exchange

   B   Standard for deferred payment

   C   Store of value

   D   Unit of account [1]

5 What is the opportunity cost of saving?

   A   Borrowing

   B   Earning interest

   C   Paying interest

   D   Spending [1]

Total: [5]

Chapter 16
Households

LEARNING INTENTION

By the end of this chapter, you will be able to:
- analyse the influences on households' spending, saving and borrowing.

KEY TERMS

consumer durables · consumption · disposable income · mortgage · rate of interest · savings rate/ratio · wealth

Key skills activities

1 Table 16.1 shows the different amounts that may be spent, saved or borrowed by households at four different income levels. Complete the table and explain whether the pattern you find between the different income levels and spending, saving and borrowing is the expected one.

Table 16.1: Spending, saving and borrowing at different income levels

Disposable income ($)	Spending ($)	Saving ($)	Borrowing/dissaving
10 000	13 000	0	
26 000	24 000		0
52 000		6 000	0
120 000	70 000		0

SELF-ASSESSMENT

How confident did you feel completing Activity 1? Think about the points below. Then decide whether you would award your understanding a gold medal, a silver medal or a bronze medal.

- Was the pattern between disposable income, spending and saving the one you expected to see?
- Do you understand how some people are able to spend more than they earn?

 Strong understanding – able to be a coach, that is able to explain the topic to another student

 Good understanding – but stronger understanding of some aspects of the topic needed to reach gold standard

 Some understanding – but need to review most aspects of the topic

2   Table 16.2 lists four possible reasons for saving. Match the following four people with an appropriate reason for saving.

- A 16-year-old student
- A 25-year-old who is getting married
- A 40-year-old with two children
- A 60-year-old about to retire.

Table 16.2: Different people's reasons for saving

Reasons for saving	Person
To buy a house	
To pay future medical bills	
To pay university fees	
To provide a financial safety net	

TIP

Remember that while the rich are likely to save more of their income than those on low incomes, it is likely to be a smaller percentage.

3   Households, firms and the government may borrow. Link each decision-maker with a reason why they are likely to borrow.

Decision-maker
Firm
Government
Household

Reason why likely to borrow
Spending more than income
Spending more than revenue
Spending more than tax revenue

4   You are an economist employed by the government. The finance minister would like you to advise them on whether you expect household savings rate to increase or decrease. You collect information from surveys that suggest a lack of confidence and data that indicates incomes will rise in the future and that the rate of interest is likely to fall. The finance minister tells you that there are plans to reduce the tax on the income earned from saving. In your notebook, write a short report for the finance minister.

Chapter 16 practice questions

Circle the correct answer to each question.

1 Which type of household is likely to save the most?

   A   A high-income household with a large number of children

   B   A high-income household with a small number of children

   C   A low-income household with a large number of children

   D   A low-income household with a small number of children [1]

2 What is **not** a motive for household saving?

   A   To be able to consume more products now

   B   To cope with unexpected expenses

   C   To ensure a comfortable retirement

   D   To gain a financial return [1]

3 What is the most likely reason why a rise in the interest rate may cause a household to save less?

   A   It is experiencing a loss of confidence

   B   It is experiencing a rise in income

   C   It is saving in case of emergencies

   D   It is saving to buy a car [1]

4 Which person is most likely to find it easiest to repay a loan?

   A   Someone who has borrowed to buy a refrigerator

   B   Someone who has borrowed to enlarge a swimming pool

   C   Someone who has borrowed to expand a successful firm

   D   Someone who has borrowed to pay for a foreign holiday [1]

5 A person has disposable income of $35 200. They spend $38 500 and borrow $2 600. What are their savings?

   A   −$1 900

   B   −$700

   C $2 600

   D $3 300 [1]

Total: [5]

Chapter 17
Workers

LEARNING INTENTIONS

By the end of this chapter, you will be able to:

- analyse the wage and non-wage factors that influence an individual's choice of occupation

- discuss, using demand and supply diagrams, the influences on wage determination: demand and supply of labour, trade unions and their relative bargaining power, government policy

- explain the reasons for differences in wages

- discuss how the reasons for differences in wages influence the wages of workers

- explain the causes and consequences of changes in the occupational and geographical mobility of labour

- define the division of labour (worker specialisation)

- discuss the advantages and disadvantages of division of labour.

KEY TERMS

collective bargaining   division of labour   earnings
elasticity of demand for labour   elasticity of supply of labour
national minimum wage (NMW)   mobility of labour   primary sector
real income   sector   secondary sector   specialisation   strike
tertiary sector   trade union   wage differential   wage rate

Key skills activities

1. Place the 20 words and phrases in the word cloud into five groups of four connected words/phrases and state how they are connected. Some words/phrases may fit into more than one group. However, there is only one solution that will give five groups of connected words/phrases. Complete the grid on the next page.

| Surgeon   Car park attendant   Generous pension |
| Job security   Paid national minimum wage (NMW)   Company car |
| High pay   Long holidays   Press for wage rises |
| Take industrial action   Inelastic demand   Long lunch break |
| Protect workers' rights   Use subsidised canteen   First-class train travel |
| Inelastic supply   Medical insurance resist redundancies |
| Weak bargaining power |

Word group			Connection

SELF-ASSESSMENT

How confident did you feel completing Activity 1? Think about the points below. Then see if you can construct a similar activity for other students based on workers in the primary, secondary and tertiary sectors.

- Do you know two payments a worker may receive in addition to their basic wage?

- Do you understand how non-wage factors may attract more workers to a particular occupation?

2 Complete the crossword using the clues below. You can download the crossword grid from GO (Worksheet 17.2).

Across

1 A term for workers specialising in particular tasks. (8, 2, 6)
5 An influence on the power of a trade union. (4)
9 The sector someone would work in if they are employed in agriculture, fishing, forestry or mining. (7)
10 The opposite of the public sector. (7)
11 Workers would want these in terms of holidays but not in terms of working hours. (4)
12 An acronym for a wage rate that firms cannot legally pay below. (3)
13 What a government does to 12 across. (3)
14 A key influence on the wage paid to a worker. (6)
15 A highly paid occupation that may involve working in a court. (6)
18 A description of work which involves very physical labour or difficult mental tasks. (4)
19 A break from work. (7)
20 A highly paid occupation working with animals. (3)
21 An extra benefit a worker may receive. (6)
22 A payment to labour. (4)

Down

2 Concentration on a narrow range of products or tasks. (14)
3 The type of mobility involving changing jobs. (12)
4 The strength of a worker or trade union in negotiating with an employer. (10, 5)
6 These workers are usually highly paid. (7)
7 A reward to workers. (3)
8 The manufacturing and construction sector. (9)
10 Payments made by a government or firms to retired workers. (8)
13 Safety from being made redundant. (8)
15 What workers may become when they lose motivation. (4)
16 The effect an increase in the supply of workers may have on their wage rate. (6)
17 Trade .... – an organisation that represents workers. (5)

3 Either individually or in a pair, rank the following five workers from the highest paid to the lowest paid. Write an explanation for your choice and explain two additional pieces of information that it would have been useful to have in making your decision.

- Worker A: Data processing analyst, age 25, with a degree in mathematics, employed by a successful commercial bank.
- Worker B: Farm worker, age 40, with no academic qualifications.
- Worker C: Neurosurgeon, age 45, with a doctorate in medicine.
- Worker D: Accountant, age 55, employed in a foreign insurance firm based in the country who has a degree in business studies.
- Worker E: Assembly line worker, age 35, with two IGCSEs, working in a biscuit factory packaging products.

Write your answers in your workbook.

> **TIP**
>
> It would be useful to find an example of a well-paid occupation and a low-paid occupation in your country and the reasons for the differences in their wages. This should help you understand the influences on the differences on wages. You may also be able to use these examples in answers to questions on this topic.

4 Decide whether the changes shown in Table 17.1 would increase or decrease geographical mobility of labour. Include a brief explanation for your decision.

Table 17.1: Geographical mobility of labour

Change	Decrease/increase geographical mobility of labour	Reason for increase/decrease
Decrease in information about job vacancies		
Decrease in differences in house prices and rents throughout the country		
Improvement in healthcare in the capital city		
Improvement in internet connection		
Improvement in train travel		

5 Division of labour can bring advantages and disadvantages to consumers, firms and workers. Complete Table 17.2 with one possible advantage and disadvantage for each group.

Table 17.2: Advantages and disadvantages of labour

Group	Possible advantage	Possible disadvantage
Consumers		
Firms		
Workers		

Chapter 17 practice questions

Circle the correct answer to each question.

1 In which situation would the demand for labour be inelastic?

    A   Demand for the product produced is elastic

    B   It is difficult to replace workers with machines

    C   It takes a short time to train new workers

    D   There is high unemployment in the economy [1]

2 The diagram shows the market for bus drivers.

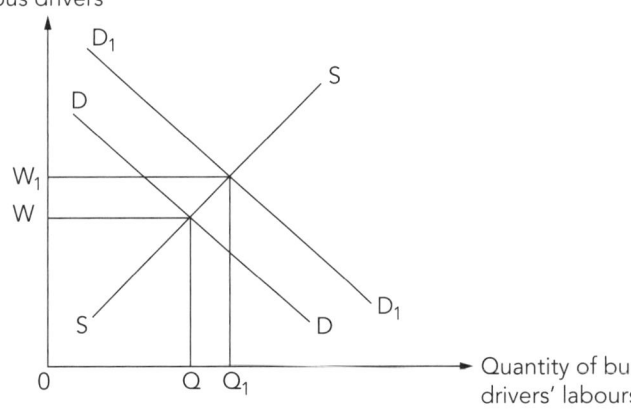

17 Workers

What change could have caused the change in the wage rate paid to bus drivers?

A   A decrease in the qualifications needed to be a bus driver

B   A decrease in the wage paid to train drivers

C   An improvement in the bus drivers' working conditions

D   An increase in bus travel [1]

3   What could cause an extension in the supply of farm workers' labour?

A   A decrease in the dangers included in farm work

B   A decrease in the number of hours farm workers have to work

C   An increase in the non-wage benefits received by farm workers

D   An increase in the wage rate paid to farm workers [1]

4   Which change in the nature of a job would be most likely to increase the number of people willing to do it?

A   A decrease in holiday entitlement

B   A decrease in job satisfaction

C   An increase in job insecurity

D   An increase in on-the-job training [1]

5   What would strengthen the power of a trade union?

A   Demand for the product produced by the workers is elastic

B   It is difficult to substitute the workers by machines

C   Its members are unwilling to take industrial action

D   The wages form a high proportion of the industry's total cost [1]

Total: [5]

> Chapter 18
Firms

LEARNING INTENTIONS

By the end of this chapter, you will be able to:

- explain the difference between primary, secondary and tertiary sector firms
- explain the difference between private sector firms and public sector firms
- discuss the advantages and disadvantages of small firms and large firms
- define the different types of mergers: horizontal, vertical and conglomerate
- discuss the advantages and disadvantages of mergers
- discuss how internal and external economies and diseconomies of scale can affect a firm/industry as the scale of production changes
- draw and interpret average total cost (ATC) diagrams to illustrate economies and diseconomies of scale.

KEY TERMS

conglomerate merger   external economies of scale
external diseconomies of scale   external growth
horizontal merger   industry   internal diseconomies of scale
internal economies of scale   internal growth   rationalisation
vertical merger   vertical merger backwards
vertical merger forwards

Key skills activities

1. Complete Table 18.1 to give a summary of the primary, secondary and tertiary industries.

   Table 18.1: Primary, secondary and tertiary industries

Industry	Involved in	Example
Primary	Extracting raw materials	
Secondary		Furniture
Tertiary		

18 Firms

2 Complete Table 18.2 by deciding whether the following workers are likely to be employed by primary, secondary or tertiary firms and private sector or public sector firms.

Table 18.2: Employment in different types of industries and different sectors

Workers	Primary/secondary/ tertiary firms	Private sector/public sector firms
Farm worker		Private
Fast food delivery driver		
Jewellery maker		
Police officer		

3 A small carpet firm applies to the bank for a loan. In your notebook, write a short report to the bank outlining the possible challenges facing the small firm and how it may be able to compete with large rival carpet firms.

SELF-ASSESSMENT

How confident did you feel completing Activity 3? Think about the points below. Then circle the traffic light you have reached.

- Do you know two advantages a small firm may have in comparison to a large firm?

- Do you understand why a commercial bank may be more willing to lend to a large firm than to a small firm?

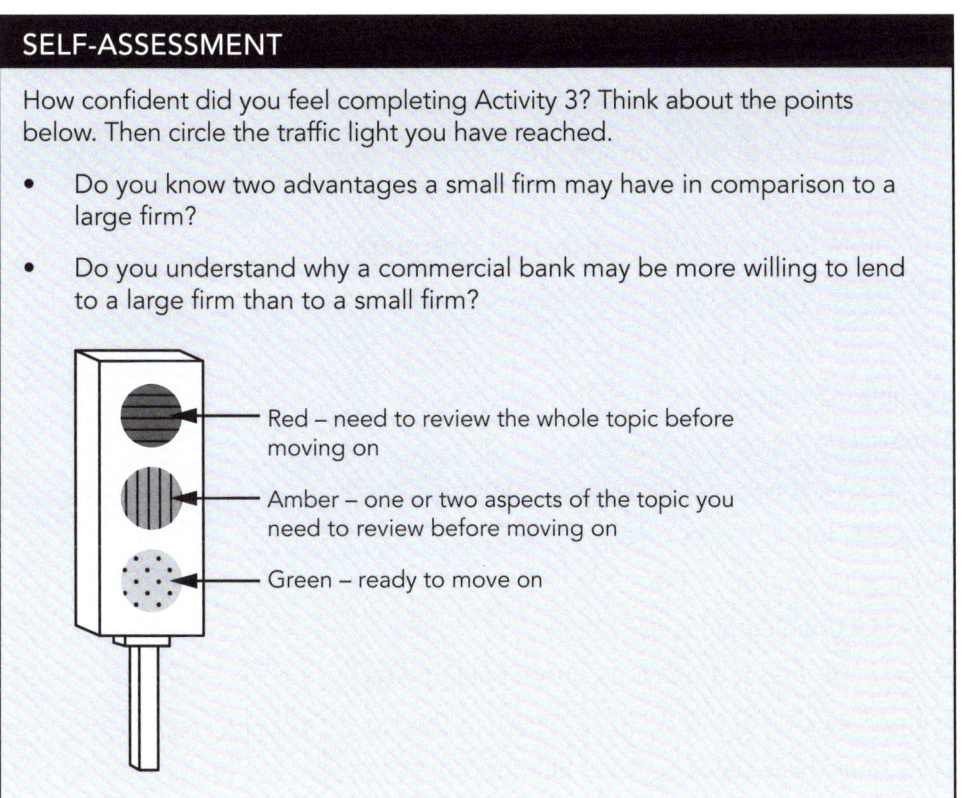

Red – need to review the whole topic before moving on

Amber – one or two aspects of the topic you need to review before moving on

Green – ready to move on

CAMBRIDGE IGCSE™ AND O LEVEL ECONOMICS: WORKBOOK

 4 Complete the crossword using the clues below. You can download the crossword grid on GO (Worksheet 18.4).

Across

1. A merger between firms producing different products. (12)
5. A type of economy of scale related to workers concentrating on different parts of producing a good or service. (6)
7. A type of economy of scale related to employing specialist workers. (10)
8. Size of firms that may exist if technical economies of scale are not important. (5)
9. The type of economies of scale that arise due the growth of an industry. (8)
13. The type of economies of scale that arise due to the growth of a firm. (8)
15. The sector involved in providing services. (8)
16. The firms which are able to take advantage of economies of scale that arise due to the growth of the industry. (3)
21. Example of an internal diseconomy of scale. (10, 8)
22. A merger between firms at different stages of the production of a product. (8)
23. A disadvantage of a firm or an industry growing too large. (12)
24. A type of internal economy of scale. (10)
25. What will be happening to a firm's average cost as it expands if it experiences economies of scale. (7)

Down

1. What may be of poorer quality if a firm gets too large. (13)
2. Two or more firms combining. (5)
3. Which firms in an industry can take advantage of the industry growing in size. (3)
4. The sector which includes agriculture. (7)
6. Term used to describe buying a large quantity. (4)
10. Average cost if total cost is $4 500 and output is 450. (3)
11. What a firm hopes its customers will do even if rival firms enter the industry. (4)
12. A type of internal economy of scale. (9)
14. Which firms producing cars would be included in the car industry. (3)
17. Another name for a subsidy. (5)
18. An economy of scale that may be gained by a firm producing a variety of products. (4, 7)
19. Another name for buying economy of scale. (10)
20. The sector controlled by the government. (6)

18 Firms

5 Firms may merge at the same or different stages of production. Use arrows to show the direction of the different types of merger in Figure 18.1. Examples have been done for you.

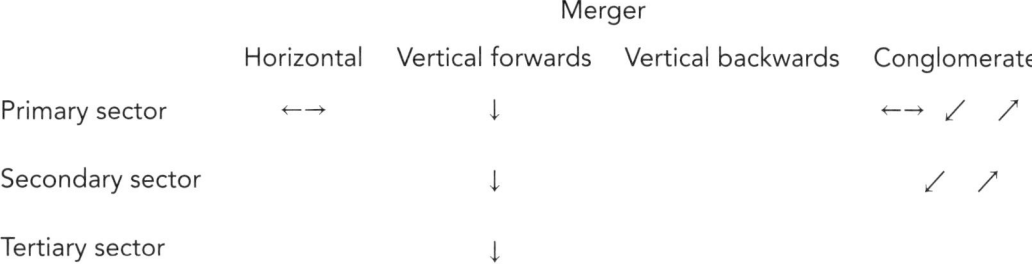

Figure 18.1: Types of mergers

6 As an airline and a car manufacturer increase in size, each may benefit from economies of scale. Complete Table 18.3 with examples of the economies of scale they could benefit from. Some examples have been completed for you.

Table 18.3: Economies of scale

Economies of scale	Increase in size of an airline	Increase in size of a car manufacturer
Buying/purchasing	Fuel bought in bulk	
Financial		Greater ease of obtaining a bank loan
Labour	Employ baggage workers who specialise in finding lost luggage	
Managerial		
Marketing	Advertise at football matches	
Risk bearing		
Selling	Reduced cost of transporting inflight meals to airport	
Technical	Use of wide-body aircraft (Jumbo jets)	

TIP

Remember, economies of scale are concerned with a fall in average cost and not total cost. As a firm grows in size, it would be expected that its total cost will rise.

87

Chapter 18 practice questions

Circle the correct answer to each question.

1 What may stop a firm growing in size?

   A   A lack of finance to expand

   B   Low cost of transport to consumers

   C   The existence of economies of scale

   D   The large size of the market [1]

2 Which type of merger aims to ensure control of retail outlets?

   A   Conglomerate

   B   Horizontal

   C   Vertical backwards

   D   Vertical forwards [1]

3 Which economy of scale is an external economy?

   A   Ability to buy raw materials in bulk

   B   Ancillary industries providing goods and services for the industry

   C   Costs reduction achieved by using more efficient machines

   D   More efficient use of the skills of workers [1]

4 Which feature is an advantage of small-scale production?

   A   Diversification

   B   Division of labour

   C   Economies of scale

   D   Flexible production [1]

5 What can cause internal economies of scale?

   A   A firm's costs rising by more than its output

   B   A reduction in a firm's productive efficiency

   C   A rise in the number of firms in the industry

   D   An increase in the size of a firm's factories [1]

Total: [5]

> Chapter 19
Firms and production

> **LEARNING INTENTIONS**
>
> By the end of this chapter, you will be able to:
>
> - analyse the influences on the demand for factors of production
> - analyse the reasons for adopting labour-intensive production or capital-intensive production
> - discuss the advantages and disadvantages of different forms of production
> - explain the difference between production and productivity
> - explain the influences on production and productivity
> - analyse the effects of changes in investment on productivity.

> **KEY TERM**
>
> corporate income (corporation) tax

Key skills activities

1. Complete the mind map on Worksheet 19.1 to show the causes of a change in the demand for labour. You can download the mind map from GO.

2. Complete the sentences below using words from the box.

capital	capital-intensive	complements	derived
easier	efficient	hours	less	product
productivity	skilled	substitutes

   a. A rise in the price of capital may increase demand for labour if capital and labour are .... However, it may decrease demand for labour if capital and labour are ....

   b. Labour productivity would increase if output falls by .... than the number of .... worked.

c Advances in technology which reduce the price of .... goods and make it .... to use them encourage the adoption of .... methods of production.

d Demand for a factor of production is a .... demand. This means that it is demand for the .... produced.

e Production may increase while .... falls if a high number of less .... workers are employed, or a greater quantity of less .... capital equipment is used.

3 Producers may choose to use labour-intensive methods or capital-intensive methods. Complete Table 19.1 to give a summary of the two methods.

Table 19.1: Capital-intensive and labour-intensive production

	Capital-intensive production	Labour-intensive production
Definition	Production that uses a high proportion of capital relative to labour	
Advantage		Handmade products may be of a high quality
Disadvantage	May break down	
Example		Hospitality

> **TIP**
>
> It is very important not to confuse production and productivity. An increase in productivity is often a cause of an increase in production but it is possible for the two to move in opposite directions.

4 All the changes below may increase labour productivity. However, there is a possibility that they may not. In each case, write an explanation of why the change may increase labour productivity and why it might not.

a Increased government spending on education.

b Investment in capital goods that may incorporate new technology.

c Increased government spending on healthcare.

d Reduction in working hours.

e Increase in hybrid working, that is spending some time in the firm's place of work and some time at home.

Write your answers in your notebook.

> **SELF-ASSESSMENT**
>
> How confident did you feel completing Activity 4? Think about the points below. Then try explaining one of your answers to a partner, bringing out the difference between production and productivity.
>
> - Do you know the key influences on factors of production?
> - Are you able to explain the differences between capital-intensive production and labour-intensive production?
> - Do you understand why it is important to be clear on the difference between production and productivity?

Chapter 19 practice questions

Circle the correct answer to each question.

1. What is likely to be a feature of an industry using capital-intensive production methods?

    A   High concentration on personal services

    B   High set-up costs

    C   Low barriers to entry

    D   Low proportion of capital employed [1]

2. The table shows how the output of a firm changes as more workers are employed. At what level of employment is productivity at its highest?

Number of workers	Total output (units)
5	200
6	270
7	350
8	416
9	450

    A   6 units

    B   7 units

    C   8 units

    D   9 units [1]

3 What is most likely to result in a decrease in labour productivity?

   A A decrease in the health of workers

   B A decrease in the proportion of workers without a university degree

   C An increase in the quality of the training given to workers

   D An increase in worker motivation due to better industrial relations [1]

4 What effect would the employment of more workers, who are less well qualified than those initially employed, have on production and productivity?

	Production	Productivity
A	decrease	decrease
B	decrease	increase
C	increase	increase
D	increase	decrease

[1]

5 Why might the introduction of more advanced capital equipment by a firm not increase its output?

   A The capital equipment costs more than the annual wage bill

   B The capital equipment is a complement to labour and not a substitute for labour

   C Workers are not adequately trained to use the capital equipment

   D Workers are not resistant to the introduction of more advanced capital equipment [1]

Total: [5]

> Chapter 20

Firms' costs, revenue and objectives

LEARNING INTENTIONS

By the end of this chapter, you will be able to:

- define key terms: total cost (TC), average total cost (ATC), fixed cost (FC), average fixed cost (AFC), variable cost (VC), and average variable cost (AVC)

- calculate total cost, average total cost, fixed cost, average fixed cost, variable cost and average variable cost

- draw and interpret diagrams that show how changes in output can affect costs of production

- define total revenue (TR) and average revenue (AR)

- calculate total revenue and average revenue

- explain the influence of sales on revenue

- discuss the objectives of firms including survival, social welfare, profit maximisation and growth.

KEY TERMS

average fixed cost (AFC)		average revenue (AR)
average total cost (ATC)		average variable cost (AVC)
fixed cost (FC)	long run	price	profit maximisation
short run	total cost (TC)	total revenue (TR)

Key skills activities

 1 Download the crossword grid from GO (Worksheet 20.1) and complete it using the clues below.

Across

1   The full cost of producing a given output divided by that output. (7, 5, 4)

7   Equivalent to total revenue divided by sales. (5)

9   The direction of an AFC curve. (4)

12 The name for materials such as cotton used to produce a good. (3)

14 What average variable cost is if variable cost is $3 000 and output is 300. (3)

16 What fixed cost is if total cost is $120 and total variable cost is $110. (3)

17 The full cost of producing a good or service. (5, 4)

18 What average fixed cost is if average total cost is $11 and average variable cost is $5. (3)

21 What average variable cost is if total variable cost is $60 and output is 30. (3)

22 The objective of staying in the industry. (8)

24 Output that is sold. (5)

27 Average revenue multiplied by the quantity sold. (5, 7)

29 A description of the total fixed cost curve. (8)

31 What variable cost is when output is zero. (4)

32 A type of costs that will be high in firms that are not capital-intensive. (6)

Down

2   Total cost minus fixed cost. (8, 4)

3   This type of cost is another name for average total cost. (7)

4   Average revenue when total revenue is $240 and sales are 30. (5)

5   What output is if total fixed cost is $80 and average fixed cost is also $80. (3)

6   The objective of making as much profit as possible. (6, 12)

8   The objective of benefiting society. (6, 7)

10 What is divided into total cost to give average total cost. (6)

11 What average variable cost is if average fixed cost is $7 and average total cost is $16. (4)

13 Another name for average total cost. (4)

15 The objective of increasing the size of the firm. (6)

19 The quantity of a product that a firm has sold if its total revenue is $270 and average revenue is $30. (4)

20 What happens to AFC as output increases. (4)

23 What average fixed cost is if output is 20, total cost is $300 and average variable cost is $11. (4)

25 The size of firms that are likely to have the lowest AFC. (5)

26 What a firm experiences when total cost is greater than total revenue. (4)

28 Interest, a fixed cost, is paid on this. (4)

30 The cost of building this type of tower will be higher than building a short tower. (4)

31 The change in total fixed cost when one more unit is produced. (4)

2 a Figure 20.1 shows a firm's cost curves. Label the curves appropriately.

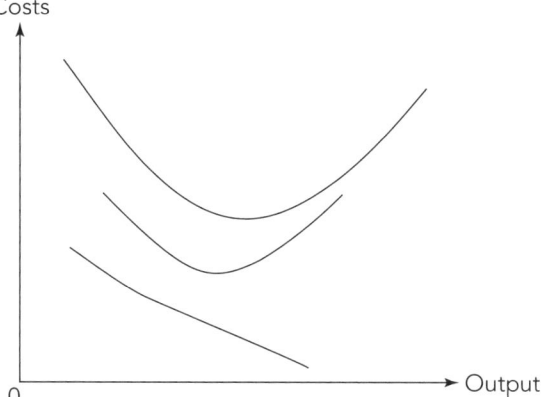

Figure 20.1: Cost curves

> **TIP**
>
> Be careful not to confuse revenue and profit. By increasing its sales, a firm may increase its revenue, but its profit will fall if revenue rises by less than its costs.

b In each case, draw a cost curve diagram to show:

i Internal economies of scale

ii External economies of scale

iii Internal diseconomies of scale

iv External diseconomies of scale.

Draw the diagrams in your notebook. You may also wish to include your diagram on revision cards on costs of production.

3 Download the sudoku grid from GO (Worksheet 20.3) and complete it. Each row, column and square should be filled out with the numbers 1 to 9, not repeating any numbers within a row, column or square. Answering questions a–f will provide you with six figures to fill in.

a If a firm sells 70 units and receives a total revenue of $210, what is average revenue?

b If a firm makes a profit of $2 per unit sold and the price per unit is $7, what is the average total cost?

c The total cost is $3 200 and output is 400, what is the average total cost?

d What is the total fixed cost if average fixed cost is $2 and the output is 4?

e The output is zero and total fixed cost is $200, what is the average fixed cost when output is 50?

f The average variable cost is $2 and average fixed cost is $4, what is the average total cost?

> **TIP**
>
> While it is uncertain what will happen to average total cost when output rises, total cost is always likely to rise.

SELF-ASSESSMENT

How confident did you feel completing Activity 3? Think about the points below. Then circle the number of smiley faces to show your level of confidence from 1 (need to revisit my understanding of firms' costs, revenue and objectives) to 5 (feeling very confident).

- Do you understand how costs and revenue may change as output and sales increase?
- Are you able to explain the differences between the objectives of growth and profit maximisation?

4 Complete Table 20.1 to show which motive objective – growth, profit maximisation, social welfare or survival – explains each action.

Table 20.1: Firms' objectives

Action	Objective
Cutting costs	
Merging with a less profitable rival	
Replacing plastic packaging with biodegradable paper packaging	
Seeking a bank loan	

Chapter 20 practice questions

Circle the correct answer to each question.

1 The table shows the total cost of a firm at different levels of output.

Output	Total cost ($)
0	20
1	30
2	38
3	42
4	50

What is the average fixed cost of producing five units of output?

A $4

B $12

C $20

D $60 [1]

2 Which cost is a variable cost?

A Interest payments on a bank loan

B Pensions paid to former employees

C Rent paid to a landlord

D Wages of workers paid on a piece-rate basis [1]

3 What is meant by 'fixed costs'?

A Costs that do not alter a firm's profits

B Costs that only change with output in the long run

C Total cost of raw materials

D Total cost plus variable cost [1]

4 A firm sells 30 units of output which cost $600 to produce and it makes a total profit of $150. What is the firm's average revenue?

A $5

B $15

C $20

D $25 [1]

5   What must be equal when a firm sells one unit of output?

    A   Average fixed cost and average variable cost

    B   Average revenue and total revenue

    C   Average total cost and average revenue

    D   Total cost and total revenue [1]

    Total: [5]

> Chapter 21
Types of markets

> **LEARNING INTENTIONS**
>
> By the end of this chapter, you will be able to:
>
> - explain the characteristics of a competitive market
> - discuss the advantages and disadvantages of competitive markets
> - explain the effect of having a high number of firms on price, quantity, choice and profit
> - explain the characteristics of a monopoly market
> - discuss the advantages and disadvantages of a monopoly market
> - explain the effect of having only one firm on price, quantity, choice and profit.

> **KEY TERMS**
>
> barrier to entry   barrier to exit   competitive market   market structure   monopoly   scale of production   sunk costs

Key skills activities

1 Some characteristics of a competitive market have benefits for consumers. Complete Table 21.1 with a benefit to consumers for each of the possible characteristics.

Table 21.1: The benefits to consumers of a competitive market

Possible characteristic	Benefit to consumers
Choice	
Low price	
High number of firms	
High quality	

2 Download the mind map from GO (Worksheet 21.1) and complete it to give a summary of the causes, characteristics and consequences of a monopoly.

> **SELF-ASSESSMENT**
>
> How confident did you feel completing Activity 2? Think about the points below. Then produce five quiz questions on different types of markets. You could try these out on another student.
>
> - Would you be able to draw a mind map on a competitive market?
> - Are you able to explain the possible advantages and disadvantages of both types of markets?

3 Download the crossword grid from GO (Worksheet 21.2) and complete it using the clues below.

Across

1   An arrangement where many buyers and sellers exchange a product. (11, 6)

6   Costs which cannot be recovered if a firm leaves an industry. (4)

9   What a firm earns when revenue is greater than cost. (6)

10 A business organisation. (4)

11 How the amount of choice in a monopoly compares with that which exists in a competitive market. (5)

12 What exists when there are a number of competing firms in a market. (6)

17 The direction in which the supply curve of a competitive market will move if more firms enter the market. (5)

18 How the profit of a firm in a competitive market may compare to that of a monopoly. (4)

20 The number of competitors a monopoly may have. (4)

22 A product in a competitive market will have a number of these. (11)

23 An acronym for average total cost. (3)

25 Entry into a competitive market will be this. (4)

27 A description of a firm that competes with another firm. (5)

28 Revenue minus profit. (4)

Down

2   Two firms joining together. (6)

3   Introduction of new products and new methods of production. (10)

4   The only firm in the market. (8)

5 An acronym of total cost. (2)

7 A description for competition existing in a natural monopoly. (8)

8 Whether profit arises before or after costs have been deducted. (5)

10 An acronym of fixed cost. (2)

13 What the profit will be when revenue is high and cost is low. (4)

14 Legal protection of an invention. (6)

15 A possible objective of a firm. (6)

16 What firms do not want to happen to their share of the market. (4)

19 What there may be a barrier to in a monopoly. (5)

21 What may be high in a competitive market. (7)

24 What happens to profit when revenue decreases while cost rises. (4)

26 An acronym of average fixed cost. (3)

> **TIP**
>
> Many monopolies are large firms, especially if they are the result of mergers or driving rivals out of the market. However, a monopoly does not have to be large. It may be small if the market is small. So, if you give as an advantage of a monopoly the ability to enjoy economies of scale, make clear that this would only be the case if the monopoly is a large firm.

Chapter 21 practice questions

Circle the correct answer to each question.

1 A market consisted of 30 firms ten years ago. It now consists of four firms. What could explain this decline in the number of firms in the market?

   A   Conglomerate mergers

   B   Horizontal mergers

   C   Reduction in barriers to entry

   D   Reduction in start-up costs [1]

2 What is a reason why a firm may wish to eliminate other firms in the industry?

   A   To experience diseconomies of scale

   B   To gain greater market share

   C   To increase the price elasticity of demand for its product

   D   To reduce the price elasticity of supply of its product [1]

3 Why might the quality of products be high in a monopoly market?

   A Ability to keep potential rival firms out of the market

   B Ability to spend a high amount on research and development

   C Strong bargaining power, which can keep raw material cost low

   D Strong bargaining power, which can keep wage costs low [1]

4 What does a central bank have a monopoly in?

   A Charging interest on loans

   B Employing public sector workers

   C Giving advice to the government

   D Issuing bank notes [1]

5 In a region of a country, there is one Portuguese restaurant, 30 restaurants serving Chinese food and 50 restaurants serving Indian food. What can be concluded about the following markets in the region?

	Portuguese restaurants	Chinese restaurants	Indian restaurants	All restaurants
A	monopoly	monopoly	monopoly	competitive
B	monopoly	monopoly	competitive	competitive
C	monopoly	competitive	competitive	competitive
D	competitive	competitive	competitive	monopoly

[1]

Total: [5]

Section 3 practice questions

1 Read the source material carefully before answering all parts of the question.

India fact file	2022
Population	1.42bn
GDP per head	$2 411
GDP growth (% GDP)	7.0
Current account of the balance of payments (% GDP)	−2.0

A savings rate is the proportion of disposable income not spent on consumption. In other words, it is the percentage of disposable income that is saved. The savings rate is much higher in Asia than in Europe and North America. Where average incomes are low, it can be expected that the savings rate will be low, although this is not always the case. Taking a wider view, low savings mean less funding is available for investment in the economy.

Table 1 shows variations in the savings rate for selected Asian economies.

Table 1: Household savings rate for selected Asian economies, 2022

Cambodia	34%	Korea	37%
China	45%	Malaysia	26%
Indonesia	33%	Philippines	20%
India	30%	Thailand	27%
Japan	30%	Vietnam	33%

Figure 1 shows the savings rate for the East Asian and Pacific region. It includes the economies shown in Table 1.

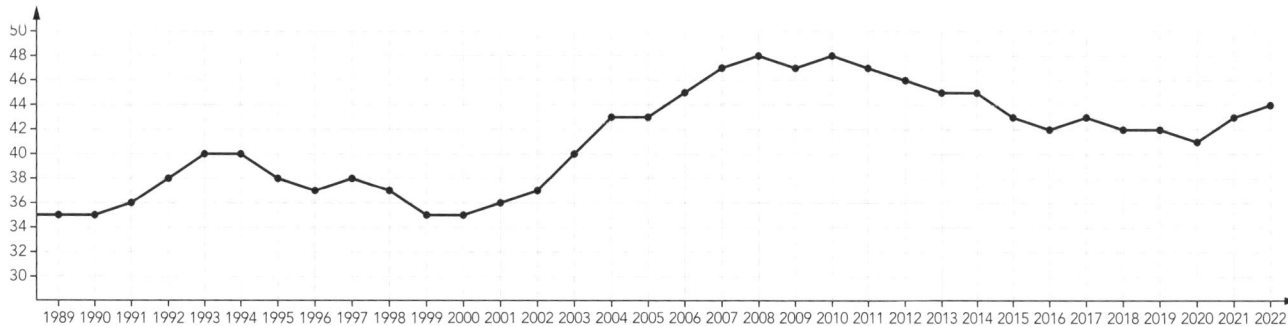

Figure 1: Household savings rates, East Asia and Pacific, 1989–2022

As elsewhere in the East Asia and Pacific region, households in India saved much more money than usual during the worst years of the COVID-19 pandemic, 2020–2022. When concerns over COVID-19 faded, Indian consumers went on a spending spree. There was high spending on property, apartments and new vehicles. Much of this spending was funded by borrowed money, particularly housing loans.

Credit expansion during the pandemic was supported by low interest rates designed to stimulate household consumption. These low rates though had a negative effect on household savings. Fewer funds were now available for investment in the economy. This shortage put upward pressure on interest rates, reducing private investment by firms. In the longer term, this might prove costly for India's economy. It is a situation that could occur in other East Asian and Pacific economies.

Refer to the information in the source material in your answers.

a Calculate the difference between the highest and lowest household savings rates for East Asian and Pacific countries from 1989 to 2022. [2]

b Identify how COVID-19 affected the household savings rates for East Asian and Pacific countries. [2]

c Explain **one** reason why households in East Asia and Pacific countries save money. [2]

d Explain **two** reasons for the difference in household savings rates between East Asian and Pacific countries. [4]

e Analyse how a decrease in the household savings rate affects the market for essential food items in East Asian and Pacific countries. [4]

f Discuss whether or not a high household savings rate is beneficial for economic growth in India and in other East Asian and Pacific countries. [6]

Total: [20]

> **TIP**
>
> Part d is about differences in the household savings rates. It involves comparing one country with another or comparing groups of countries. Words like 'higher' and 'lower' should make this clear. Avoid simply repeating data from the table.

Improve this answer

Here is a sample answer to part d:

1 *The data indicates significant differences between countries, notably between China and the Philippines. There are fewer variations between other countries with savings ratios falling between 27% and 33% of disposable income. Social reasons are a very likely source of differences. There are likely to be differences in attitude towards savings. In Cambodia, for example, savings may be required to meet household needs such as paying for healthcare, while in Vietnam, which has a higher savings ratio, there may be more help from the government with childcare or higher pension payments, allowing households to use savings to purchase 'big ticket' items.*

2 *Disposable income is also important. As it rises, the proportion devoted to savings increases. This probably applies when comparing one country with another one.*

Section 3 practice questions

> **YOUR CHALLENGE**
>
> See whether you can improve this answer. Before you write your answer, think about the points below:
>
> - Both reasons for the differences in household savings are relevant. Differences in attitudes towards saving are clearly explained with good reference to the source material.
> - The second reason is OK but is vague and too short. More content is required drawing upon the data and referring to income differences.

2 The largest container vessel ever built was launched in 2023. It has been designed to carry thousands of containers of manufactured goods from China to Western Europe. The problem faced by its owner is that due to high fixed costs, the benefits from economies of scale only apply when the vessel is working at or close to its capacity.

   a Define 'economies of scale'. [2]
   b Explain **two** examples of economies of scale. [4]
   c Analyse the effects of high fixed costs on a firm's output and prices. [6]
   d Discuss whether or not consumers benefit from economies of scale. [8]

   Total: [20]

> **TIP**
>
> Remember to refer to the information in the source material in your answers. You may also find it useful to refer to other examples you have studied.

> **WORKED EXAMPLE ANSWER FOR PART B**
>
> As a firm increases its scale of operations, there are various ways in which long run average total costs fall. This is referred to as the benefits from economies of scale.
>
> In the case of a container vessel, as the capacity to carry containers increases, the average cost of transporting a container falls. This can give a vessel's owners a competitive edge over other firms in the market. The typical cost of moving a garment from China to Europe is now less than 50 cents due to technical economies of scale in their transportation.
>
> A second example of economies of scale is financial. Large firms find it easier to obtain loans from banks, as they are able to provide security to a lender. Small firms are going to be more restricted. Large firms are also able to obtain loans at a lower rate of interest as they are less likely to default on the repayments. The result is a reduction in long run average total costs for large firms.

> **TIP**
>
> The worked example answer for part b consists of two cases of internal economies of scale. An alternative example of external economies of scale could have been used. But remember that the question only asks for two examples.

3 Read the source material carefully before answering all parts of the question.

Thailand fact file	2022
Population	71.2m
Unemployment rate	0.9%
Labour force participation rate	66.7%
Adult literacy rate	93.8%

Thailand is the second largest economy in Southeast Asia. It has experienced an average rate of economic growth of 3.8% over the past 20 years as well as two periods of deep recession (1997 and 2008).

Table 2 shows some key labour market statistics for 2022.

Table 2: Average monthly salary by profession and location of employment

Profession	
Hospital doctor	$6 750
Business development manager	$4 590
Human resources manager	$4 500
Software developer	$2 843
Teacher	$2 520
Real estate agent	$2 088

Location	
Thailand average, of which:	$2 787
Bangkok*	$3 317
Chiang Mai*	$3 168
Phuket*	$1 925

*Principal cities

The average monthly salary includes any monetary compensation that is paid, for example, for housing, transportation and personal insurance. It varies between professions on account of experience, age and educational qualifications. For example, a worker with a university degree can expect to earn 24% more than a worker with a professional diploma. The average salary also varies between cities. Firms in Bangkok and Chiang Mai pay more than in Phuket where the main employment is in tourism and hospitality. For many individual workers, non-wage reasons can explain why that person may not always take the highest paid job on offer.

Thailand is one of the few Southeast Asian countries to have a national minimum wage. In 2022, this was around $10 per day, well below the average monthly income. The minimum wage is not popular with trade unions although most workers on a minimum wage would argue that it reduces the possibility of exploitation by a strong employer.

Section 3 practice questions

Refer to the information in the source material in your answers.

a Calculate the opportunity cost in dollars ($) when a Thai software developer becomes a teacher. [2]

b Identify **two** possible non-wage reasons why the software developer has decided to become a teacher. [2]

c Explain how the market system determines the salary of a teacher in Thailand. [2]

d Explain **two** reasons why the average monthly income in Bangkok differs from that in Phuket. [4]

e Analyse why there is a difference in the average salary of hospital doctors and HR managers in hospitals in Thailand. [4]

f Discuss whether or not workers in Thailand have benefited from the introduction of a national minimum wage. [6]

Total: [20]

WORKED EXAMPLE ANSWER FOR PART E

It is usual to assume that the higher the demand and the lower the supply of workers in an occupation, then annual pay is likely to be higher. This can be seen from the data in the table where the salary difference between a hospital doctor and an HR manager is $250 each month.

Supply is the key consideration. The supply of hospital doctors is likely to be low compared to HR managers. Doctors require essential qualifications before they can practise. These qualifications take time, require extensive training and cost a lot of money. An HR manager will also require professional qualifications but at a lower level and requiring less time to complete.

The diagram explains the salary difference.

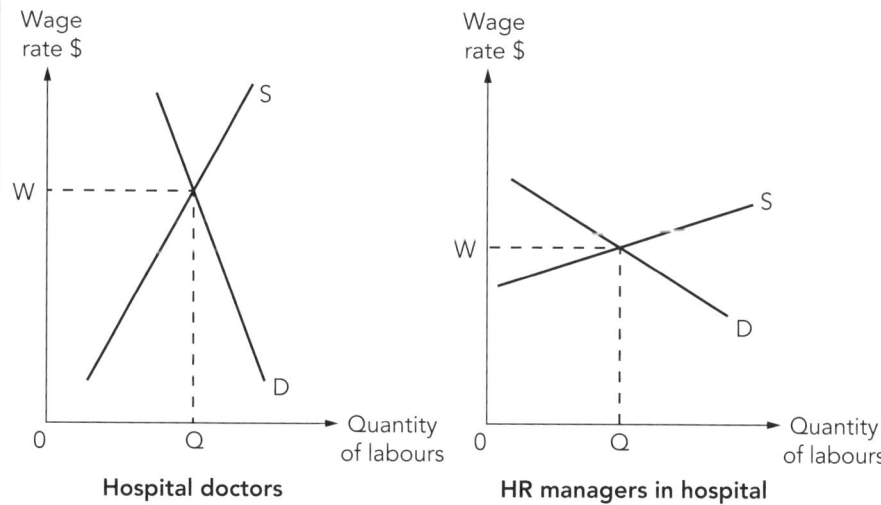

The demand and supply of doctors is inelastic. In contrast, for HR managers, demand and supply are more elastic.

CAMBRIDGE IGCSE™ AND O LEVEL ECONOMICS: WORKBOOK

4   Singapore has almost 600 supermarkets. NTUC Fair Price and Dairy Farm International Retail Group are the two largest firms with a market share of over 50% of supermarket sales. Both firms have grown through mergers and acquiring other firms. There is still a place in the market for small locally owned supermarkets and convenience stores.

   a   Define a 'merger'. [2]

   b   Explain two reasons why firms decide to merge. [4]

   c   Analyse the effects of having only one firm on price, quantity, choice and profit in a market. [6]

   d   Discuss whether or not small firms are able to compete in competitive markets. [8]

   Total: [20]

> **TIP**
>
> The mark allocation for the part b question is 4 marks. This represents about 10 minutes' writing time. In this case, a clear diagram supports the example answer, although a good answer could be produced without using a diagram. If you are unclear what the diagram should show, it is better not to use up valuable time trying to produce one.

Improve this answer

Here is a sample answer to part d:

In any type of economy, the small firm is the normal form of business. This particularly applies in service sector markets such as shops, restaurants, hotels and personal services such as healthcare and hairdressing.

Firms tend to be small if the size of the market is small. Small firms dominate food provision in my country. Nearly all restaurants are family-owned. As well as size, small firms tend to compete in local markets. Many owners may not want their firm to grow. They are happy to stay in business provided they can have a decent living.

Small firms cannot always compete due to the power of larger firms. These can dominate a market and can control price and quality. This can drive small firms out of a market although they are sometimes bought up by large firms.

An exception is in the case of a pharma firm I know. This small firm has developed a new form of treatment for a skin problem and been able to patent it. This made it a target for one of our big pharma companies which is hoping to make a lot of money from its takeover.

> **YOUR CHALLENGE**
>
> See whether you can improve this answer. Before you write your answer, think about the points below:
>
> - This answer has some valid points and contains relevant examples from a market known to the student.
> - The main weakness is that the answer is written in a descriptive style. The improved answer should be more analytical and include economic terms to replace more general description. There is scope to extend the examples, but these should be written in a less informal way.

Section 4
Government and the macroeconomy

Chapter 22
Government macroeconomic intervention

LEARNING INTENTIONS

By the end of this chapter, you will be able to:

- explain the macroeconomic aims of economic growth, full employment/low unemployment, stable prices/low inflation, balance of payments stability, redistribution of income and environmental sustainability
- analyse the reasons behind the choice of aims
- explain the criteria that governments may set for meeting each aim
- discuss the possible conflicts between macroeconomic aims.

KEY TERMS

actual economic growth   aggregate demand (AD)
aggregate supply (AS)   balance of payments
economically active   economically inactive   full employment
inflation   inflation rate   potential economic growth
stable prices

Key skills activities

1 Link each term to its correct definition.

Term
Balance of payments
Economic growth
Full employment
Inflation

Definition
An increase in the output of an economy and, in the long run, an increase in the economy's productive potential.
The record of a country's economic transactions with other countries.
The rise in the average price level of goods and services over time.
The lowest level of unemployment possible.

22 Government macroeconomic intervention

2 The Government of Country A has an inflation rate target of 3%, and Country B has an inflation rate target of 8%. Decide which of the following could justify Country B having a higher inflation rate target and write an explanation of your decision in your notebook.

a Country B has a record of high inflation.

b Country B's inflation rate is higher than Country A's.

c Country A's inflation rate is rising while Country B's inflation rate is falling.

d Country B's government raises state benefits, including unemployment benefit and pensions, in line with inflation while Country A's government does not.

e Country A produces mainly tertiary products, whereas Country B produces mainly agricultural products.

TIP

It would be useful to find out what your government's macroeconomic aims are, as you may be able to use this information to support your answers.

SELF-ASSESSMENT

How confident did you feel completing Activity 2? Think about the points below. Then circle the medal to show your level of understanding of government macroeconomic intervention.

- Are you able to explain the main government macroeconomic aims?
- Would you be able to explain why the aim of economic growth may conflict with the aim of environmental sustainability?

Gold: Strong understanding – able to be a coach, that is able to explain the topic to another student

Silver: Good understanding – but stronger understanding of some aspects of the topic needed to reach gold standard

Bronze: Some understanding – but need to review most aspects of the topic

3 You are in charge of a school kitchen that is planning to double the number of meals served to students. Write a brief proposal outlining two ways the kitchen could double the meals it serves. Remember there is a risk that increasing output may damage the environment, so your plan needs to be environmentally sustainable.

Chapter 22 practice questions

Circle the correct answer to each question.

1 What is most likely to increase people's living standards?

   A   A decrease in the country's inflation rate from 3% to −1%

   B   A decrease in the country's international competitiveness

   C   An increase in the country's economic growth rate from 4% to 6%

   D   An increase in the country's unemployment rate from 5% to 8%   [1]

2 What is meant by 'stable prices'?

   A   A constant inflation rate of 6%

   B   A low and constant rise in prices

   C   A zero percentage price change

   D   The same number of products falling in price as rising on price   [1]

3 What is the aim of a government redistributing income from the rich to people living in poverty?

   A   A more uneven distribution of income

   B   An even distribution of income

   C   A greater reduction in the income of the rich than of people living in poverty

   D   A reduction in the gap between the income of the rich and people living in poverty   [1]

4 Why is it impossible to achieve 0% unemployment?

   A   Some people will be changing jobs

   B   Some people will be in higher education

   C   Some people will be joining the labour force

   D   Some people will be leaving the country   [1]

5 Which two government aims are likely to benefit from an increase in total (aggregate) demand?

   A   Higher current account deficit and lower inflation rate

   B   Higher economic growth rate and lower unemployment rate

   C   Higher inflation rate and higher unemployment rate

   D   Lower current account surplus and lower inflation rate   [1]

Total: [5]

Chapter 23
Fiscal policy

LEARNING INTENTIONS

By the end of this chapter, you will be able to:

- define government budget, budget deficit and budget surplus
- calculate the size of a government budget deficit or surplus
- explain the main areas of government spending
- analyse the reasons for and effects of government spending
- analyse the reasons for taxation: raising revenue, discouraging consumption of demerit goods, reducing imports, redistributing income, influencing total demand, encouraging environmental sustainability
- explain the different classifications of tax: progressive, regressive, proportional, direct and indirect
- analyse the impact of taxation on consumers, workers, firms/producers, government and the economy
- define fiscal policy
- analyse taxes and government spending changes in the form of fiscal policy measures
- discuss how fiscal policy measures may enable a government to achieve its macroeconomic aims.

KEY TERMS

contractionary fiscal policy   direct taxes   expansionary fiscal policy
flat taxes   government budget   government budget deficit
government budget surplus   indirect taxes   multiplier effect
national debt   progressive tax   proportional tax   regressive tax

Key skills activities

1   Calculate:
  a   The government budget position when government spending is $384bn and government revenue is $297bn
  b   Government spending when there is a government budget surplus of $1 250bn and government revenue is $4 200bn
  c   Government revenue when there is a government budget deficit of $65bn and government spending of $535bn

d   Government spending when there is a balanced government budget and government revenue is $34 572bn

e   The government budget balance when government spending is $40 500bn and government revenue is $41 510bn

Then use your answers to match the figures with the letters in the grid to find the name of a country that has one of the largest economies in the world. Add up your answers to parts a–e. Use this figure to match.

1	2	3	4	5	6	7	8	9
A	B	C	D	E	F	G	H	I
J	K	L	M	N	O	P	Q	R
S	T	U	V	W	X	Y	Z	

Country: ....

 2   Download the crossword grid from GO (Worksheet 23.2) and complete it using the clues below.

Across

1   The main source of government revenue. (3, 7)

6   Objectives a government may have for the macroeconomy. (4)

8   Changes in government spending and taxation. (6, 6)

10 Business organisations that produce goods and services. (5)

11 The type of demand influenced by government macroeconomic policy. (5)

13 Adjusted for inflation. (4)

14 A type of tax that takes a larger percentage of the income of those with a high income than those with a low income. (11)

16 A certain quantity or amount. (4)

18 This is caused by government spending exceeding government revenue. (6, 7)

21 A tax on goods and services. (6)

22 Differences between import tariff and import duty. (4)

24 A tax on goods and services. (8)

25 What a government spends money on in order to reduce it or prevent it. (5)

26 A government does this to the tax rate on firms' profit. (3)

27 Fiscal policy may be used to achieve environmental .... (14)

Down

2   A main area of government spending. (9)

3   A possible reason for taxation. (14)

4   A reward for labour or what households and firms have to do when taxes are imposed on them. (3)

5   A tax with just one rate regardless of income. (4)

7   What the government budget position is if government revenue exceeds government spending. (7)

9   A tax which takes the same percentage of the incomes of people with both high and low incomes. (12)

12 How government spending on defence compares to government spending on education in most countries. (4)

13 A tax that takes a higher percentage of the income of those with low income than those with high income. (10)

15 What a government may do to tax rates to increase total demand. (6)

17 Who carries out fiscal policy. (5)

19 An example of an indirect tax. (3)

20 Goods and services bought from other countries. (7)

21 Goods that a government may tax in order to discourage consumption. (7)

23 16 across. (4)

3   A government is considering spending $2bn more on education. In a pair, produce a podcast in which you cover:

   a   The possible opportunity cost of spending more on education

   b   The benefits of higher government spending on education.

4   Link each tax to the correct reason for imposing the tax.

Tax
Excise duty on cigarettes
Excise duty on petrol
GST/VAT
Progressive personal income tax
Tariff

Reason for imposing the tax
Encourage environmental sustainability
Influence total demand
Redistribute income
Reduce consumption of a demerit good
Reduce imports

5   Decide whether each of the following personal income tax systems are progressive, proportional or regressive and give a reason why. Complete Table 23.1.

Table 23.1: Different types of personal income tax systems

Tax paid on an income of $10 000	Tax paid on an income of $50 000	Tax paid on an income of $100 000	Type of tax and reason
$2 000	$10 000	$20 000	
$1 000	$12 500	$40 000	
$3 000	$10 000	$15 000	

6   Download the flowchart from GO (Worksheet 23.6) and complete it to give a summary of how the expansionary fiscal policy measure of cutting the rates of personal income tax may reduce unemployment.

> **TIP**
>
> Remember, whether a tax system is progressive, proportional or regressive depends not on the amount of tax different income groups pay but on the percentage of their income they pay in tax.

> **SELF-ASSESSMENT**
>
> How confident did you feel completing Activity 6? Think about the points below. Then produce a leaflet on contractionary fiscal policy that could be used by other students.
>
> - Are you able explain the difference between a budget deficit and a budget surplus?
> - Would you be able to construct a flowchart on how contractionary fiscal policy could reduce inflation?

Chapter 23 practice questions

Circle the correct answer to each question.

1   Which policy would be classified as a fiscal policy measure?

   A   A cut in the rate of interest

   B   An increase in the money supply

   C   A rise in government spending on defence

   D   The imposition of a quota   [1]

23 Fiscal policy

2 Which economic problem may cause a government to cut taxation?

- A A current account deficit
- B A high, unsustainable rate of economic growth
- C Cyclical unemployment
- D Demand-pull inflation [1]

3 What is a disadvantage of a progressive system of income tax?

- A It discourages the growth of the informal economy
- B It may act as a disincentive to work
- C It may increase the mobility of labour
- D It redistributes income for those living in poverty to the rich [1]

4 A government increases its spending on benefits for those living in poverty and raises the top rates of direct taxes. What does this suggest is its main aim?

- A Balance of payments stability
- B Economic growth
- C Stable prices
- D Redistribution of income [1]

5 A government wants to encourage firms to expand production.
Which combination of policy measures may achieve this objective?

	Corporate income tax (corporation tax)	Income tax
A	decrease	decrease
B	decrease	increase
C	increase	increase
D	increase	decrease

[1]

Total: [5]

Chapter 24
Monetary policy

LEARNING INTENTIONS

By the end of this chapter, you will be able to:

- define monetary supply and monetary policy
- explain monetary policy measures: changes in money supply, interest rate and foreign exchange rate
- discuss the effect of monetary policy on government macroeconomic aims.

KEY TERMS

contractionary monetary policy   expansionary monetary policy
foreign exchange rate   interest rate
monetary policy   money supply

Key skills activities

1 An increase of the interest rate will have an effect on the following. Decide in each case whether an interest rate rise will cause an increase or a decrease. Write the answers in your notebook.

   a   Consumer expenditure

   b   Cost of borrowing

   c   Investment

   d   Reward for saving

   e   Total demand.

 2 Download the wordsearch grid from GO (Worksheet 24.2) and find the words related to monetary policy.

| exchange rate | expansionary | interest | investment |
| monetary policy | money supply | saving | total demand |

TIP

If you need to explain how one monetary policy measure works, the interest rate is a useful one to select. The links between changes in the interest rate and macroeconomic aims are relatively straightforward.

3 Download the mind map from GO (Worksheet 24.3) and complete it to give you a summary of monetary policy.

> **SELF-ASSESSMENT**
>
> How confident did you feel completing Activity 3? Think about the points below. Then see if you can produce one revision card on monetary policy and one revision card comparing monetary policy and fiscal policy.
>
> - Are you able to identify the three monetary policy measures?
> - Are you able to explain the difference between an expansionary monetary policy and a contractionary monetary policy?

Chapter 24 practice questions

Circle the correct answer to each question.

1 Which policy measure is an example of monetary policy designed to reduce total (aggregate) demand?

   A A limit placed on bank lending

   B A reduction in interest rates

   C A rise in income tax

   D A switch in government spending from consumer to capital goods [1]

2 What is an example of an expansionary monetary policy measure?

   A A decrease in government spending on central bank buildings

   B A decrease in the rate of an indirect tax

   C An increase in government spending on central bank workers' wages

   D An increase in the country's money supply [1]

3 A government introduces a contractionary monetary policy. What is most likely to be its aim?

   A Lower economic growth rate

   B Lower inflation rate

   C Lower interest rate

   D Lower unemployment rate [1]

4 What do fiscal policy and monetary policy have in common?

    A   They both include changes in interest rates

    B   They both include changes in tax rates

    C   They both seek to influence the government budget balance

    D   They both seek to influence total (aggregate) demand   [1]

5 What is likely to be the main aim of a central bank?

    A   Environmental sustainability

    B   High government revenue

    C   Price stability

    D   Profit   [1]

Total: [5]

Chapter 25
Supply-side policy

> **LEARNING INTENTIONS**
>
> By the end of this chapter, you will be able to:
>
> - define supply-side policy
>
> - explain supply-side policy measures: education and training, infrastructure spending, labour market reforms, lower direct taxes and improving incentives to work and invest, deregulation, privatisation and subsidies
>
> - discuss the effects of supply-side policy on government macroeconomic aims.

KEY TERMS	
deregulation	supply-side policy

Key skills activities

1   **a**   Use the letters in the outer circle to form the name of a supply-side policy measure. The letters can be used more than once.

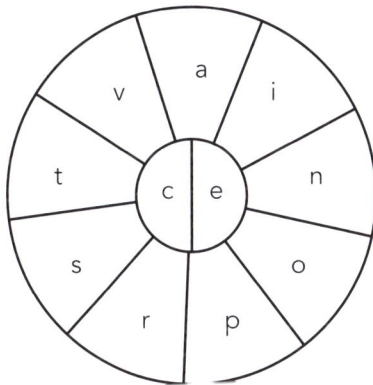

Supply-side policy measure: ....

b   Use some of the letters in the outer circle plus the two letters in the inner circle to form another word. This word is what may be provided to workers by a cut in direct taxes. Again, the letters may be used more than once.

....

2 Download the crossword grid from GO (Worksheet 25.2) and complete it using the clues below.

Across

1   A supply-side policy measure which may encourage firms to increase their investment. (3, 9, 3)
3   A macroeconomic aim. (6)
6   An item that a government may increase its spending on to reduce firms' costs of production. (14)
9   To spend money on capital goods. (6)
10 An increase in the efficiency of mining this product would increase South Africa's economic growth rate. (4)
11 A name for the difference between low wages and unemployment benefit. (3)
14 The type of tax that may be reduced to provide a greater incentive to work and invest. (6)
16 A government payment to encourage firms to increase their output. (7)
18 A type of infrastructure. (4)
19 What will have happened to productivity if supply-side policy is successful. (5)
20 Differences in this may reduce geographical mobility of labour. (4)
21 What supply-side policy may try to do the labour market. (6)
23 What supply-side policy will try to do to industrial action. (4)
24 What supply-side policy aims to make costs. (3)
25 If education is of poor quality, the opportunity to raise productivity will be ………………………….. (4)
26 What supply-side policy seeks to increase. (5, 6)

Down

2   A supply-side policy measure designed to increase workers' skills. (8)
4   Supply-side policy may try to cut …………………………. uncompetitive practices. (3)
5   The opposite of nationalisation. (13)
7   The currency of Brazil. (4)
8   Something a supply-side policy measure aims to reduce. (4)
12 Output per worker hour. (12)
13 A piece of equipment used in the production of pottery. (4)
15 An organisation that will be affected by labour market reforms. (5, 5)
16 A form of industrial action. (7)
17 The type of outcome any government policy measure aims to achieve. (4)
21 What deregulation removes. (5)
22 Revenue minus profit. (4)

25 Supply-side policy

3 Decide whether the supply-side policy measures will be likely to increase the role of market forces or the role of the government in the economy. Complete Table 25.1.

Table 25.1: The effect of supply-side policy measures on the role of market forces and government

Supply-side policy measure	Increase role of market forces or government
Construction of new state railway	
Deregulation	
Introduction of a national minimum wage	
Lower personal income tax rates	
Privatisation	
Reduction in trade union rights	
Reduction in unemployment benefit	
State grants to private sector firms to spend on training workers	

> **TIP**
>
> In deciding whether a cut in taxes and an increase in government spending is a supply-side policy measure or fiscal policy measure, consider what is the main objective. If the objective is to increase total supply, it is a supply-side policy measure. If it is to increase total demand, it is a fiscal policy measure.

SELF-ASSESSMENT

How confident did you feel completing Activity 3? Think about the points below. Then circle the traffic light you have reached.

- Are you able to explain the main objective of supply-side policy?
- Are you able to analyse how three supply-side policy measures may help a government achieve its macroeconomic aims?

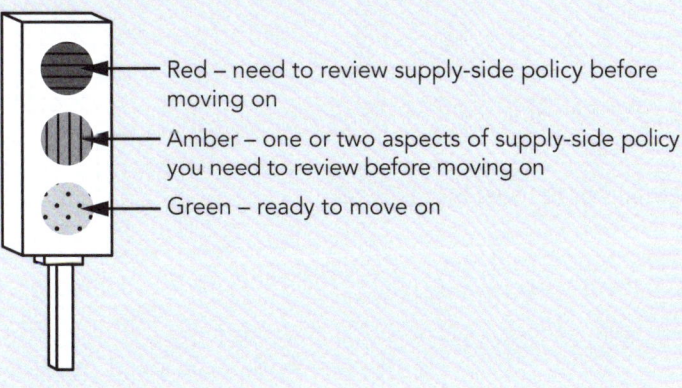

- Red – need to review supply-side policy before moving on
- Amber – one or two aspects of supply-side policy you need to review before moving on
- Green – ready to move on

4 In a pair, produce a podcast on whether you think an increase in government spending on education would increase total supply in your country.

Chapter 25 practice questions

Circle the correct answer to each question.

1. Which supply-side policy measure may a government take to encourage firms to expand and multinational companies (MNCs) to set up branches in the country?

    A   A cut in corporation tax

    B   A cut in spending on training

    C   An increase in indirect taxation

    D   An increase in restrictions on bank lending [1]

2. Which might encourage more people to continue working past their retirement ages?

    A   A cut in personal income tax

    B   A cut in wages

    C   An increase in state pensions

    D   An increase in working hours [1]

3. Which supply-side policy measure may increase government revenue in the short run but may decrease it in the long run?

    A   Deregulation

    B   Government spending on infrastructure

    C   Government spending on training

    D   Privatisation [1]

4. Which organisation is most likely to oppose labour market reforms that reduces the period of notice an employer has to give before dismissing an employee?

    A   Central bank

    B   Commercial bank

    C   Multinational company

    D   Trade union [1]

5. The effectiveness of a supply-side policy would be reduced by a lack of

    A   a time lag.

    B   market failure.

    C   spare capacity.

    D   total demand. [1]

Total: [5]

Chapter 26
Economic growth

> **LEARNING INTENTIONS**
>
> By the end of this chapter, you will be able to:
>
> - define economic growth
>
> - explain how economic growth is measured: real gross domestic product (GDP)
>
> - analyse the causes of economic growth: an increase in total demand, an increase in the quantity of resources or an increase in the quality of resources
>
> - discuss the advantages and disadvantages of economic growth
>
> - define a recession
>
> - analyse the causes of a recession: a decrease in total demand, a decrease in the quantity of resources or a decrease in the quality of resources
>
> - discuss the consequences of a recession for consumers, workers, producers/firms and the government
>
> - discuss the range of policies available to promote economic growth and their effectiveness.

> **KEY TERMS**
>
> circular flow of income   gross domestic product (GDP)
> informal economy   International Monetary Fund (IMF)
> nominal GDP   real GDP   recession   subsistence agriculture
> sustainable economic growth   transfer payments   value added

Key skills activities

 1 Download the sudoku grid from GO (Worksheet 26.1) and complete it. Each row, column and square should be filled out with the numbers 1 to 9, not repeating any numbers within a row, column or square. Answering questions a–e will provide you with five figures to fill in.

   a The economic growth rate when money GDP increases by 7% and the inflation rate is 5%.

   b The economic growth rate when real GDP increases from $800bn to $840bn.

c   The change in real GDP in $bn if the economic growth rate was 1.6% and real GDP was initially $500bn.

d   The economic growth rate when real GDP increases from $3 500bn to $3 605bn.

e   A government's economic growth rate target if it states that it wants real GDP to rise from $400bn to $416bn.

 2   Download the wordsearch grid from GO (Worksheet 26.2) and find the words related to monetary policy.

advances in technology	better climate	better education
better healthcare	higher retirement age	investment
larger labour force	rise in total demand	

3   In a pair, produce a podcast on the benefits you think your country could gain from high economic growth but also some of the risks that may be involved.

4   How might each of the following government policy measure promote economic growth? Complete Table 26.1. One row has been done for you.

Table 26.1: Government policy measures to promote economic growth

Government policy measure	How measure may promote economic growth
Cut in corporate tax rate	
Increase government spending on education	
Increase government spending on infrastructure	Reduce costs of production
Lower personal income tax rate	
Remove restrictions on immigration	

SELF-ASSESSMENT

How confident did you feel completing Activity 4? Think about the points below. Then explain to another student how one policy measure could increase economic growth in your country.

- Are you able to explain three causes of economic growth, three advantages of economic growth and three disadvantages?
- Are you able to analyse how both demand-side policies and supply-side policy may be used to promote economic growth?

TIP

In examining the effects of economic growth and a recession, remember that not everyone may be affected in the same way.

Chapter 26 practice questions

Circle the correct answer to each question.

1 What is a possible disadvantage of economic growth?

   A Environmental improvement

   B Extra consumer goods produced

   C Higher tax revenue

   D Structural unemployment [1]

2 Which changes may result in sustained economic growth?

	Total (aggregate) demand	Total (aggregate) supply
A	decrease	decrease
B	decrease	increase
C	increase	increase
D	increase	decrease

[1]

3 What is likely to increase during a recession?

   A Consumer expenditure

   B Inflation

   C Investment

   D Unemployment [1]

4 What is the most likely reason why a government budget deficit may decrease during a period of economic growth?

   A Export revenue may rise and import expenditure may fall

   B Government spending on education will fall and indirect tax rates will increase

   C Import expenditure will increase by less than export revenue

   D Tax revenue will rise and government spending on benefits may fall [1]

5 What is most likely to threaten sustainable economic growth?

   A The burning of fossil fuels

   B The preservation of rainforests

   C The reduction of traffic congestion

   D The use of wind power [1]

Total: [5]

Chapter 27
Employment and unemployment

> **LEARNING INTENTIONS**
>
> By the end of this chapter, you will be able to:
>
> - define employment, unemployment and full employment
> - explain how unemployment is measured
> - analyse the causes of unemployment: frictional, structural, cyclical and seasonal
> - discuss the consequences of unemployment for the individual, producers/firms, the government and the economy
> - discuss policies to reduce unemployment and their effectiveness.

> **KEY TERMS**
>
> causal unemployment   cyclical unemployment   economically active
> economically inactive   employment   flexible labour force
> frictional unemployment   Labour Force Survey
> labour force participation rate   regional unemployment
> search unemployment   seasonal unemployment   structural unemployment
> technological unemployment   unemployment   unemployment rate

Key skills activities

1 Calculate:

   a The number of people employed if there are 32m people of working age, 8m of whom are economically inactive and 5m are unemployed

   b The unemployment rate if 2m people are unemployed out of a labour force of 40m

   c The number of people unemployed if the population is 41m, the labour force is 20m and the unemployment rate is 5%

d The size of the labour force if a government achieves its unemployment target of 3% with 0.54m people unemployed

e The number of people unemployed if the labour force is 50m and there are 47m people employed

f The unemployment rate if 1.6m people are unemployed out of a labour force of 20m.

Then use your answers to match the figures with the letters in the grid to find the name of a type of unemployment.

1	2	3	4	5	6	7	8	9	10	11	12	13
A	B	C	D	E	F	G	H	I	J	K	L	M
14	15	16	17	18	19	20	21	22	23	24	25	26
N	O	P	Q	R	S	T	U	V	W	X	Y	Z

Employment type: ....

2 Complete the sentences below using words from the box.

> achievable   changing   cut   cyclical   decrease
> deficit   expansionary   frictional   higher   long
> longer   methods   structural   technology
> unemployment benefits

TIP

Remember that the labour force includes both employed and unemployed workers.

a An increase in total (aggregate) demand should reduce .... unemployment but may not reduce .... and .... unemployment.

b Zero unemployment is not .... as some people will always be .... jobs.

c The effects of unemployment will be more serious, the .... the unemployment rate and the .... the duration of the unemployment.

d An increase in unemployment may result in a government budget .... as tax revenue is likely to .... while government spending on .... is likely to rise.

e Unemployment be reduced by .... monetary policy which may involve a .... in the rate of interest.

f When people have been unemployed for a .... time, employers tend to become reluctant to employ them and some become out of date with advances in .... and working ....

3 Identify the type of unemployment with its cause. Complete Table 27.1.

Table 27.1: Different types of unemployment

Cause of a rise in unemployment	Type of unemployment
Change in the pattern of demand	
Fall in labour market information	
Fall in labour mobility	
Fall in total demand	
Rise in unemployment benefit	

4 Place the 16 words/phrases in the word cloud into four groups of four connected words/phrases and state how they are connected. Some words/phrases may fit into more than one group. However, there is only one solution that will give four groups of connected words/phrases. Complete the grid below.

> Current account deficit
>
> Cut in personal income tax rates   Cyclical   Demand-pull inflation
>
> Education   Frictional   Greater ease of hiring workers
>
> Higher output   Higher total demand
>
> Less need to provide fringe benefits
>
> Less pressure to increase wages   Less risk of industrial action
>
> Lower interest rate   Seasonal   Structural   Training

Word group				Connection

5 Download the mind map from GO (Worksheet 27.5) and complete it to give you a summary of the costs of unemployment to the individual, firms and the economy.

> **SELF-ASSESSMENT**
>
> How confident did you feel completing Activity 5? Think about the points below. Then decide whether you would be able to explain to another student why governments usually try to achieve as low an unemployment rate as possible.
>
> - Do you know how different groups may be affected by unemployment?
> - Are you able to explain the links between low unemployment and the other government macroeconomic aims?

Chapter 27 practice questions

Circle the correct answer to each question.

1 Which group is economically active?

   A Full-time students

   B Those who are officially classified as unemployed

   C Those who are too sick to work

   D Those who have retired early [1]

2 What is a cause of frictional unemployment?

   A A lack of information about job vacancies

   B A lack of total demand

   C Domestic consumers buying more imports

   D The introduction of new technology [1]

3 What type of unemployment is caused by workers changing jobs?

   A Cyclical

   B Frictional

   C Regional

   D Structural [1]

4 An increase in which variable may cause unemployment?

   A   Bank lending

   B   Disposable income

   C   Government spending

   D   Imports [1]

5 Which government measure would be most effective in reducing structural unemployment?

   A   Increasing government spending on training

   B   Increasing the rates of unemployment benefit

   C   Reducing income tax

   D   Reducing the rate of interest [1]

   Total: [5]

Chapter 28
Inflation

> **LEARNING INTENTIONS**
>
> By the end of this chapter, you will be able to:
>
> - define inflation and deflation
> - explain how inflation is measured using the consumer price index (CPI)
> - analyse the causes of inflation: demand-pull and cost-push
> - discuss the consequences of inflation for consumers, workers, producers/firms and the economy
> - discuss the range of policies available to control inflation and their effectiveness.

> **KEY TERMS**
>
> consumer prices index (CPI)   cost-push inflation   deflation
> demand-pull inflation   disinflation   hyperinflation
> index-linking   inflation   menu costs   monetarists
> monetary inflation   shoe-leather costs   wage-price spiral

Key skills activities

1. Download the sudoku grid from GO (Worksheet 28.1) and complete it. Each row, column and square should be filled out with the numbers 1 to 9, not repeating any numbers within a row, column or square. Answering questions a–e will provide you with five figures to fill in.

   a The consumer prices index (CPI) in a country rises from 150 to 153 over a period of a year. What is the rate of inflation?

   b If the inflation rate was 4% and nominal wages rise by 9%, what was the percentage increase in real wages?

   c If a country's inflation rate falls from 8% in 2026 to 3% in 2027, what was the rise in the price level in 2027?

   d What is the inflation rate if the consumer prices index (CPI) rises from 120 to 126?

   e The table shows the weights and the price changes of three categories of products used to construct a weighted price index. What is the change in the price level?

Item	Weight	Price change
Food	½	5
Clothing	¼	10
Leisure goods	¼	16

2   Complete Table 28.1 by deciding how each group could cause inflation and what type of inflation it would be. The first one has been done for you.

Table 28.1: Causes of inflation

Group	Action that could cause inflation	Cost-push inflation / demand-pull inflation
Consumers	Increase consumer expenditure	Demand-pull inflation
Workers		
Lenders		
Firms producing raw materials		
Government		
Government		

SELF-ASSESSMENT

How confident did you feel completing Activity 2? Think about the points below. Then produce one revision card on the causes of inflation and one revision card on the difference between cost-push inflation and demand-pull inflation for another student. You could ask them to produce two revision cards for you on another topic.

- Are you able to recognise how different groups can act in ways that may cause inflation?
- Do you know the difference between cost-push inflation and demand-pull inflation?

3   Use the internet to find a country that is experiencing inflation. Produce a poster explaining reasons why consumers, workers, savers, firms and the economy may be harmed by the inflation rate and why they may not.

TIP

Remember that inflation is a rise in the price level, so if the inflation rate stays constant at 4%, for example, it does not mean that prices have remained unchanged. Instead, it means that prices are rising at the same rate.

4 Download the flowchart from GO (Worksheet 28.4) to give a summary of supply-side policy.

5 Place the 20 words/phrases in the word cloud into five groups of four connected words/phrases and state how they are connected. Some words/phrases may fit into more than one group. However, there is only one solution that will give five groups of connected words/phrases. Complete the grid below.

> Advertising   Basket of goods and services
> Creeping   Electricity   Fiscal drag   Higher interest rate
> Higher personal income tax rates   Hyper   Increase budget surplus
> Loss of international competitiveness   Loss of purchasing power
> Menu costs   Price changes   Reduction in government spending
> Stable   Survey   Twenty percent   Transport
> Wages   Weightings

Word group				Connection

Chapter 28 practice questions

Circle the correct answer to each question.

1 A country is experiencing a high rate of inflation. Which item would be the least desirable store of wealth?

    A Land

    B Money

    C Property

    D Shares [1]

2   What circumstance would an increase in total (aggregate) demand be most likely to cause inflation?

   A   It is caused by an increase in investment undertaken by expanding industries

   B   It is the result of higher government spending on training which raises labour productivity

   C   It occurs when there is a low level of spare capacity in the economy

   D   It takes place when there is net immigration occurring   [1]

3   What is a cause of demand-pull inflation?

   A   A fall in labour productivity

   B   A fall in investment

   C   A rise in a current account deficit

   D   A rise in the budget deficit   [1]

4   In which circumstance would a rise in a country's inflation rate increase the international competitiveness of the products it produces?

   A   The country's exchange rate increases

   B   The price level of other countries increases at a more rapid rate

   C   The productivity of the country's labour force decreases

   D   The quality of the products produced by other countries improves at a more rapid rate   [1]

5   What is deflation?

   A   A rise in cyclical unemployment

   B   A fall in the economic growth rate

   C   A fall in the price level

   D   A rise in the government budget deficit   [1]

Total: [5]

Section 4 practice questions

1 Read the source material carefully before answering all parts of the question.

South Africa fact file	2023
Economic growth rate	0.2%
Labour force	24m
Unemployment rate	32%

Unemployment has been a major problem in South Africa for some time. Table 1 shows South Africa's unemployment rate between 2016 and 2023 and changes in government spending over the same period.

Table 1: Unemployment rate and changes in government spending, 2016–2023

Year	Unemployment rate (%)	Change in government spending (%)
2016	25	1.19
2017	26	1.17
2018	27	1.15
2019	28	0.57
2020	29	0.57
2021	31	0.57
2022	35	1.35
2023	32	0.34

Poor educational attainment in the country means there is a mismatch between unemployed workers and job vacancies. Many of the unemployed lack the skills required to obtain a vacancy. This problem has been made worse by periods when the total demand for goods and services in the economy has fallen. Some people who lose their jobs due to a lack of total demand, lose confidence and their skills become out of date. These two effects reduce their chances of gaining another job.

The high rate of unemployment keeps tax revenue below what it could be. South Africa has a progressive income tax system, and it is now possible for taxpayers to submit their tax forms online.

The South African government is using a range of policies to reduce unemployment. It hopes these policies will increase economic growth. In 2023, the government increased its spending on education and infrastructure.

Refer to the information in the source material in your answers.

a Calculate the number of South African workers who were unemployed in 2023. [2]

b Identify **two** costs of unemployment experienced by the South African economy and its workers. [2]

c Explain how changes in South Africa's economic growth rate can affect unemployment. [2]

d Explain **two** types of unemployment that South Africa has experienced since 2016. [4]

e Analyse the relationship between changes in the unemployment rate and changes in government spending in South Africa since 2016. [4]

f Discuss whether or not supply-side policy measures are always likely to be successful in reducing unemployment in South Africa. [6]

Total: [20]

> **TIP**
>
> Remember the formula for the unemployment rate and how it can be used to calculate the number of workers who are unemployed.

WORKED EXAMPLE ANSWER FOR PART F

There are various policies that a government can use to reduce unemployment. These are more likely to be effective when the cause of the unemployment is known.

From the information provided, it is clear that supply-side policy measures could be used. Typical measures include where funding is provided to retrain workers to acquire new skills in line with current employment needs. Updating of skills can help to meet future employment needs. Another supply-side policy is to provide better information on what jobs are available for the unemployed. Such a scheme could be linked to a policy of providing funding for unemployed workers to move to areas where there are job opportunities in line with their skills.

A second cause of job losses is due to the cyclical nature of the global economy. Total demand falls, leading to increased unemployment. For this type of unemployment, expansionary fiscal and monetary policies are the usual ways to increase total demand and so reduce cyclical unemployment.

The success of any policy is by no means certain. Much depends on whether the cause of unemployment has been correctly identified. This is not easy since there may be more than one cause of unemployment. Supply-side measures are more likely to be effective over time while fiscal measures can have a more immediate impact on reducing unemployment.

> **TIP**
>
> Part f refers to 'measures'. Your answer should include at least two supply-side measures as well as a brief explanation of one other type of policy for reducing unemployment.

2 Switzerland has traditionally come close to full employment. In 2023, it had an unemployment rate of 4.2%. The country also had a high rate of investment. In contrast, Djibouti had high unemployment, and this had been the case for some time. The Djibouti government has been trying over many years to reduce unemployment in the country.

a Define 'full employment'. [2]

b Explain **two** government macroeconomic aims, apart from full employment. [4]

Section 4 practice questions

    c   Analyse what may happen to unemployment if investment increases. [6]

    d   Discuss whether or not the unemployment of labour is more serious than the unemployment of other factors of production. [8]

Total: [20]

Improve this answer

Here is a sample answer to part b:

One government macroeconomic aim is low and stable inflation. Governments do not aim for zero inflation, as measures of inflation tend to overstate price rises. A low inflation rate may encourage producers to make more. A stable rate makes it easier for firms and households to plan for the future.

Another macroeconomic aim is for the economy to produce more. If an economy is making more goods and services, it will export more. The extra exports will increase the economy's revenue and more people can be employed producing them.

> **YOUR CHALLENGE**
>
> See whether you can improve this answer. Before you write your answer, think about the points below:
>
> - The first part is strong. It correctly identifies a macroeconomic aim and goes on to explain it.
> - The second part is not strong. It states that a macroeconomic aim is to achieve a higher output but does not recognise whether this is economic growth.
> - The answer also does not establish why exports would rise. Just because more products are made does not mean that more will be exported. There has to be demand for the exports as well as potential supply.

3   Read the source material carefully before answering all parts of the question.

India fact file	2019	2022
Population	1.38bn	1.42bn
GDP per head	$2 050	$2 411
Current account of the balance of payments	−1.1% GDP	−2.0% GDP
Life expectancy at birth	70.7 years	67.2 years

The IMF World Economic Outlook for 2024 forecast that India is likely to show significant economic growth over the period to 2028. This report estimated that India would benefit from almost constant economic growth of around 6.4% per year. The Bank of India's estimate for 2023/24 was higher at 7.3% growth. If these levels of economic growth are realised, India is on track to be the world's third largest economy by 2030. Forecast annual economic growth for the other five largest economies varied from 3.2% (China), 2% (the USA), 1.4% (the UK), 0.9% (Germany) and 0.3% (Japan).

A leading Indian economist has argued that the main reason for India's recent economic growth is increased investment by privately owned domestic firms and a surge in the net inflow of investment from foreign-owned companies. This second type of investment is called foreign direct investment (FDI) and has mainly been in the manufacturing sector, particularly in electronics, chemicals, textiles and vehicle production. Table 2 shows the acceleration in investment in 2021 and 2022 and the related change in real GDP.

Table 2: Two indicators of India's recent economic growth

Year	Investment (% change)	Real GDP (% change)
2017	7.8	6.1
2018	11.2	7.3
2019	1.6	4.6
2020	−10.4	−6.0
2021	14.6	8.9
2022	11.4	6.7

The Indian government has successfully planned to increase economic growth through additional central and state funding for infrastructure improvements. This has involved huge amounts of government spending on new motorways, upgrading commuter rail services in cities, regional airport development and improving the quality of power supplies. In some cases, projects have been in partnership with the private sector. This is an example of a supply-side policy aiming to increase India's productive potential. Other supply-side policies involve funding education and training programmes to improve the quality of India's workforce.

India's newfound economic success is not shared equally among its population, with huge differences in the distribution of income between households, particularly in cities such as Mumbai. Most rural areas have income levels way below that in cities. There are economic pressures on all households through persistent inflation, typically 6% per year, higher taxes and cutbacks in social benefits.

Recent and future projected economic growth rates will undoubtedly bring benefits to many households, workers and firms. Despite considerable progress, in 2022, around 10% of the population lived in absolute poverty. Life expectancy at birth for males and for females fell to 65.8 years and 68.9 years, respectively. The key issue is whether the high rates of economic growth will continue and whether the benefits from economic growth can be more equally distributed.

Section 4 practice questions

Refer to the information in the source material in your answers.

- **a** Calculate the percentage change in the growth of investment in India from 2020 to 2021. [2]

- **b** Calculate the average annual rate of real GDP growth over the period 2017 to 2022 and identify a year in which there was a decrease in total output in India. [2]

- **c** Explain what is meant by 'real GDP growth'. [2]

- **d** Explain **two** benefits of increasing real GDP growth for Indian households. [4]

- **e** Analyse the relationship between changes in investment and real GDP growth in India from 2017 to 2022. [4]

- **f** Discuss whether or not India is likely to continue to experience high economic growth up to 2030. [6]

Total: [20]

Improve this answer

Here is a sample answer to part e:

An increase in investment in an economy can produce an increase in economic growth. Similarly, if investment falls, it is most likely that the rate of economic growth will fall. In both cases, there is a time lag as it takes time for changes in investment to lead to changes in economic growth.

The data in the table appears to agree with this relationship. From 2017 to 2018, investment increased, as did the percentage change in real GDP. Another example is from 2020 to 2021, where both changes were negative due to the COVID pandemic. However, 2021 saw a substantial increase in both variables.

4 Egypt has a serious inflation problem. In 2023, annual inflation reached an all-time high of 40%, with food and drink prices increasing by almost 70%. This inflation has been caused by an increase in demand for goods and services due to rapid population growth and by a shortage in supply of essential imported food products. The Central Bank has stated that it will use all available monetary tools to combat this inflation.

- **a** Define inflation. [2]
- **b** Explain **two** effects of high inflation on households. [4]
- **c** Analyse **two** causes of inflation. [6]
- **d** Discuss whether or not monetary policy is the best way of reducing the rate of inflation. [8]

Total: [20]

> **WORKED EXAMPLE ANSWER FOR PART D**

The main monetary policy measure used in most countries is to change the interest rate. When there is a need to combat inflation, a rise in the interest rate is expected to reduce total demand. This will lead to less consumer spending and less investment by firms. Households and firms will have to pay more interest if they continue to borrow money. New borrowers are likely to be deterred from seeking loans. Savers, in contrast, will receive an incentive to save more. Monetary policy can be effective but it takes time for interest rate changes to be effective.

Fiscal policy can also be used to deal with inflation. This policy involves increasing taxation, decreasing government spending or a combination of both. The effect is like monetary policy – total demand is reduced as consumers have less of their income to spend on goods and services. This should ease the pressure on prices. Some fiscal policy measures such as increasing taxes can be quickly implemented.

Section 5
Economic development

Chapter 29
Living standards

> **LEARNING INTENTIONS**
>
> By the end of this chapter, you will be able to:
>
> - explain indicators of living standards: real gross domestic product (GDP) per head and the Human Development Index (HDI) and its components
> - discuss the advantages and disadvantages of real GDP per head and HDI as indicators of living standards
> - analyse the reasons for differences in living standards and income distribution within and between countries.

> **KEY TERM**
>
> Human Development Index (HDI)

Key skills activities

1. Download the flowchart from GO (Worksheet 29.1) and complete it to show the stages of changing nominal GDP into a measure of living standards.

2. Decide how the changes shown in Table 29.1 would directly affect a country's HDI value. Give a reason for each decision. Complete Table 29.1.

   Table 29.1: Causes of a change in a country's HDI value

Change	Decrease / increase / leave unchanged or uncertain	Reason
Increase in life expectancy		
Increase in population with a university degree		
Reduction in income inequality		
Rise in GDP		
Rise in population		

> **TIP**
>
> Remember when exploring living standards, it is not real GDP that is important, but rather real GDP per head.

SELF-ASSESSMENT

How confident did you feel completing Activity 2? Think about the points below. Then circle the traffic light you have reached.

- Are you able to recognise the components of the HDI?
- Do you know why economic growth does not guarantee a rise in living standards?

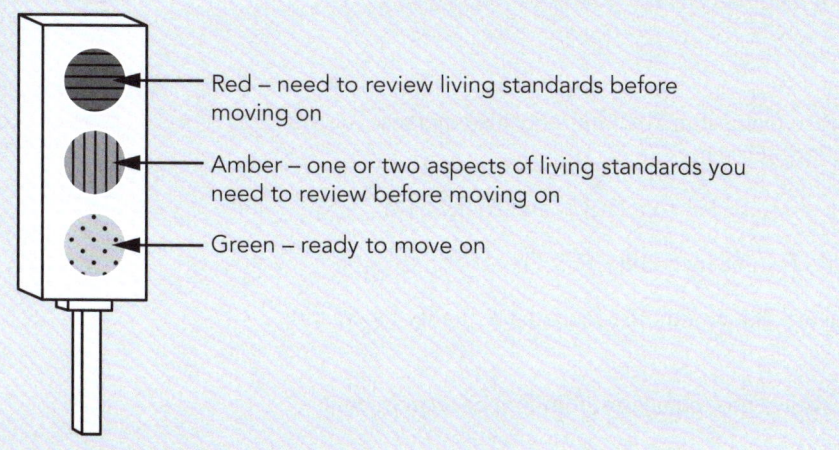

Red – need to review living standards before moving on

Amber – one or two aspects of living standards you need to review before moving on

Green – ready to move on

3 Write a script for a podcast in which you discuss whether advances in technology have increased living standards in recent years.

 4 Download the crossword grid from GO (Worksheet 29.4) and complete it using the clues below.

Across

3   An increase in the state provision of this for people may reduce income inequality. (7)

5   A high income gives a person the ability to influence this. (5)

8   Income distribution is always likely to be this. (6)

9   Short for 'Human Development Index'. (3)

10 Firms will want to do this if workers increase their skills. (6)

11 As well as income, this is also unevenly distributed. (6)

12 Short for 'National Minimum Wage'. (3)

13 What everyone's income would be if there was complete income equality. (4)

15 An HDI measure of living standards. (9)

16 The number of people who be getting an income if income is completely unevenly distributed. (3)

18 A low rate of this could increase income inequality. (9, 3)

20 People on low incomes may find it difficult to get this from a commercial bank. (4)

21 If the top rate of personal income tax moved in this direction, it would reduce income inequality. (4)

22 What might be given to a firm for producing a product for those on low incomes. (5)

23 A possible cause of wealth inequality. (11)

Down

1 Changes which may increase living standards but may also increase income inequality by creating dollar billionaires. (8, 2, 10)

2 A document outlining what will be left to relatives and friends. (4)

4 Cutting this would increase income inequality. (12, 7)

6 A supply-side policy measure that could raise income inequality by creating rich entrepreneurs. (13)

7 Unemployment among this age group may result in longer-term income inequality. (5)

14 A rise in this may increase both output and income inequality. (10)

17 Evidence of differences in income distribution is shown by differences in real GDP per .... (4)

19 Differences in this may increase income inequality. (3)

5 Now that you have attempted a number of crosswords, try constructing one of your own on an economics topic of your choice.

Chapter 29 practice questions

Circle the correct answer to each question.

1 A country has a lower real GDP per head than another country but also a smaller percentage of people living in absolute poverty. What could explain this?

   A The country has a lower population

   B The country has a lower rate of inflation

   C The country has a more even distribution of income

   D The country has more people employed in the primary sector [1]

2   A country has a low real GDP per head. What must this mean?

   A   Everyone in the country is poor

   B   Government spending on welfare benefits is high

   C   On average income levels are low

   D   There are no millionaires living in the country [1]

3   A country experiences a fall in its HDI despite a rise in life expectancy. What could explain this?

   A   A fall in access to clean water

   B   A fall in mean years of education

   C   A rise in air pollution

   D   A rise in gender inequality [1]

4   What may enable a low-income country to experience rapid economic growth?

   A   The ability to lend large amounts of domestic savings to domestic firms to spend on increasing their output

   B   The ability to take advantage of advances in technology developed by the spending on research and development in high-income countries

   C   A lack of economic growth in high-income countries

   D   A lack of unskilled workers in the primary, secondary and tertiary sectors [1]

5   What will cause a rise in a country's HDI value?

   A   Higher food consumption per head

   B   Higher income inequality

   C   Higher mean years of education

   D   Higher population size [1]

Total: [5]

Chapter 30
Poverty

> **LEARNING INTENTIONS**
>
> By the end of this chapter, you will be able to:
>
> - define and explain the difference between absolute poverty and relative poverty
>
> - analyse the causes of poverty: unemployment, low wages, illness, age and environmental factors
>
> - discuss the policies to alleviate poverty and redistribute income: promoting economic growth, improved education, improved healthcare provision, more generous state benefits, progressive taxation and national minimum wage.

> **KEY TERMS**
>
> absolute poverty   relative poverty   vicious circle of poverty

Key skills activities

1 Complete Table 30.1 to identify the difference between absolute poverty and relative poverty.

   Table 30.1: Absolute poverty and relative poverty

Indicator	Absolute or relative poverty
Insufficient income to eat in a restaurant	
Insufficient income to take a foreign holiday	
Lack of adequate clothing	
Lack of basic healthcare	
Living in three-quarters of the average housing space	
Malnutrition	

> **TIP**
>
> It would be useful to find out if your country has a measure of relative poverty, for example, households living on less than 60% of average income. You could use this information as an example in your answers.

30 Poverty

2. Place the 16 words/phrases in the word cloud into four groups of four connected words and state how they are connected. Some words/phrases may fit into more than one group. However, there is only one solution that will give four groups of connected words. Complete the grid below.

> Construction of sea defences   Economic growth
> Greater access to basic necessities   Higher incomes
> Higher unemployment benefit   Higher university fees
> Improved education   Long period of illness   More jobs
> More reliance on regressive taxes   Reduction in indirect taxes
> Retirement   Rise in incomes of the rich
> Rise in prices of basic necessities   Unemployment
> Working hours cut

Word group				Connection

SELF-ASSESSMENT

How confident did you feel completing Activity 2? Think about the points below. Then try explaining to someone who has not studied economics the difference between absolute and relative poverty and one government policy measure that could reduce both absolute and relative poverty. Explaining an economics concept to a non-specialist is a good way of assessing whether you have really understood it.

- Are you able to explain how unemployment can cause poverty?
- Do you know which groups, other than the unemployed, are most likely to experience poverty?

3 Complete the following sentences using the words in the box. A word may appear more than once.

absolute	few	income	investment	limited
living standards		low	productivity	relative
	tax	unevenly		

a A more uneven distribution of wealth would tend to lead to a more uneven distribution of ...., as wealth generates ....

b A vicious circle of poverty can be present in low-income countries with low saving leading to low ...., which in turn leads to low .... which results in low ....

c A rise in the income of those on low incomes is likely to reduce .... poverty, but .... poverty may increase if the income of the rich increases at a greater rate.

d Governments reduce income inequality by transferring some .... revenue to those on .... incomes.

e Children of those on low incomes are more likely to experience poverty as adults, as they usually have .... years of education and .... access to healthcare.

f One country may have a higher real GDP per head than another country, but most of its citizens may experience lower .... if income is very .... distributed.

 4 Download the flowchart from GO (Worksheet 30.4) and complete it to give you a summary of the effects of increased government spending on healthcare.

Chapter 30 practice questions

Circle the correct answer to each question.

1. What is meant by 'absolute poverty'?

    A   An income level that is insufficient to meet basic needs

    B   An income level that is less than 25% of the national average

    C   A lack of any income

    D   A lack of any wealth [1]

2. What could lead to a virtuous circle?

    A   Low savings

    B   Low tax revenue

    C   High imports

    D   High productivity [1]

3. Which policy measure would increase absolute and relative poverty?

    A   A cut in indirect taxes

    B   A cut in state benefits

    C   An increase in government spending on state education

    D   An increase in government spending on state healthcare [1]

4. What may cause someone to experience poverty?

    A   Better healthcare

    B   Generous state benefits

    C   Improved qualifications

    D   Loss of employment [1]

5. Why are the children of those on low incomes more likely to experience poverty than those on high incomes?

    A   Fewer health problems

    B   Fewer years of schooling

    C   Greater confidence

    D   Greater expectations [1]

Total: [5]

Chapter 31
Population

> **LEARNING INTENTIONS**
>
> By the end of this chapter, you will be able to:
>
> - define birth rate, death rate, net migration, immigration and emigration
> - explain how birth rates, death rates and net migration rates can vary between countries
> - explain the concept of optimum population
> - discuss the effects of increases and decreases in population size and changes in the age and gender distribution of population.

> **KEY TERMS**
>
> birth rate   death rate   dependency ratio
> emigration   immigration   infant mortality rate
> net immigration   net migration
> net migration rate   optimum population

Key skills activities

1 Calculate:

   a   The birth rate of a country of 28 million people that has 392 000 live births in one year

   b   The death rate of a country of 72 million people if 648 000 deaths are recorded in one year

   c   The percentage increase in population if the number of people in a country increases from 400 million to 428 million

   d   The net migration rate of a country with a population of 20 million that had a net positive migration of 100 000

   e   The net migration rate of a country with a population of 50 million that experiences net migration of 900 000.

   Then use your answers to match the figures with the letters in the grid on the next page to find the name of a country with a high birth rate.

1	2	3	4	5	6	7	8	9	10	11	12	13
A	B	C	D	E	F	G	H	I	J	K	L	M
14	15	16	17	18	19	20	21	22	23	24	25	26
N	O	P	Q	R	S	T	U	V	W	X	Y	Z

Country with high birth rate: ....

> **SELF-ASSESSMENT**
>
> How confident did you feel completing Activity 1? Think about the points below. Then try writing a multiple-choice question for another student. Write an explanation for why one option is the correct answer and why the other three are not.
>
> - Do you know the stages of calculating the different rates?
> - Do you know which changes in the different rates affect a country's population growth rate?

2   Decide whether each of the changes shown in Table 31.1 would be likely to increase or decrease a country's death rate. Give a reason for each decision. Complete Table 31.1.

Table 31.1: Causes of a change in a country's death rate

Change	Decrease/increase	Reason
Improvement in healthcare		
Increase in school-leaving age		
Increase in state pension		
Natural disaster		
Rise in nutrition		

> **TIP**
>
> Be careful to avoid confusing emigration and immigration. Emigration occurs when people exit a country, whereas immigration is when people come into a country. A quick way to remember this is by the initials EE (emigration/exit) and II (immigration/into).

3   Complete Table 31.2 with one advantage and one disadvantage of the effects of changes in population size and age structure on a country.

Table 31.2: The advantages and disadvantages of changes in population

Change in population	Advantage	Disadvantage
Fall in birth rate		
Fall in death rate		
Rise in emigration		
Rise in immigration		

4   Many countries are experiencing ageing and declining populations. These changes have both advantages and disadvantages, which are shown in Figure 31.1. Your objective is to move from Stage 1 to Stage 5 by moving from one advantage to the next advantage. The first link between Stage 1 and Stage 2 has been done for you.

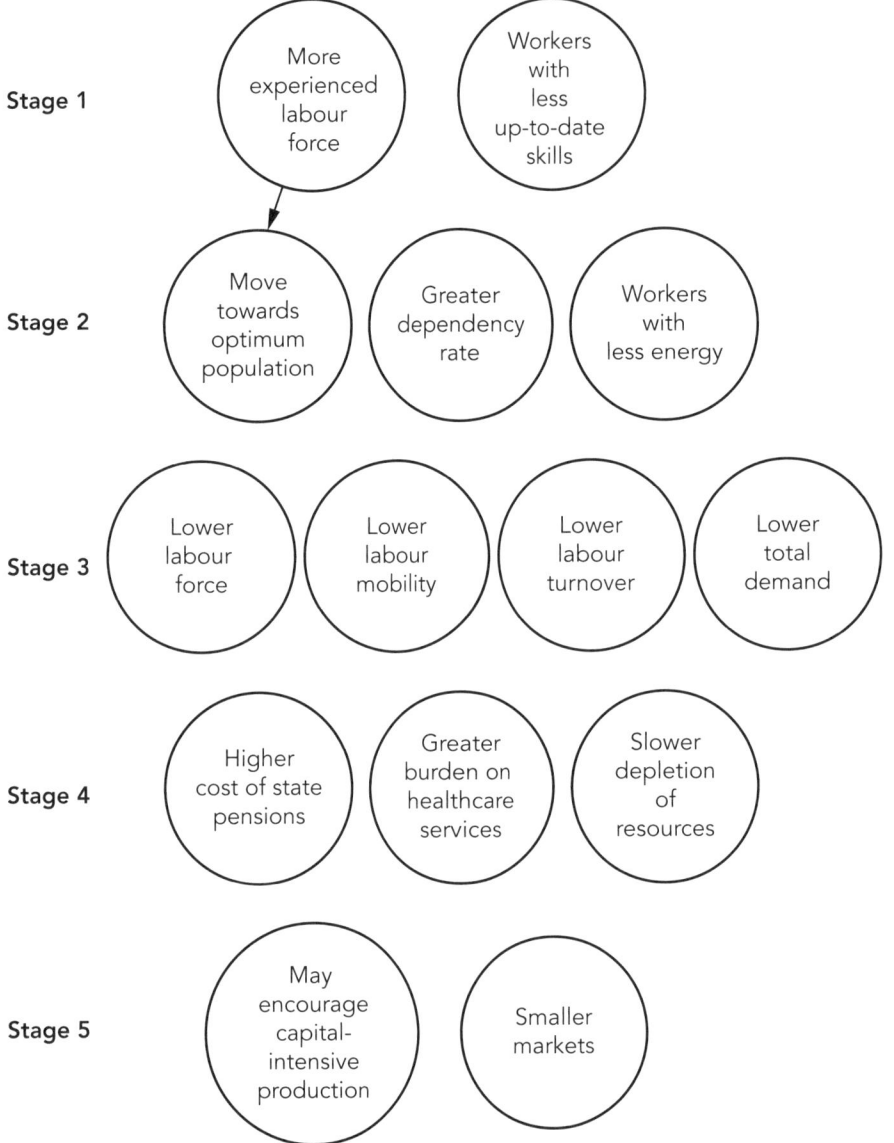

Figure 31.1: Advantages and disadvantages of ageing populations

Chapter 31 practice questions

Circle the correct answer to each question.

1   What is meant by 'a country's population growth'?

   A   The difference between a country's birth rate and death rate plus immigration

   B   The difference between a country's birth rate and death rate plus net migration

   C   The increase in a country's population in a year expressed as a percentage of the working population at the beginning of the year

   D   The increase in a country's population expressed as a percentage of world population at the beginning of the year   [1]

2   Why might a low-income country experience net immigration?

   A   It has a high and rising unemployment rate

   B   It has a low and declining real GDP per head

   C   It is surrounded by countries with more lenient immigration controls

   D   It is surrounded by even lower-income countries   [1]

3   Which change could cause a natural decrease in population?

   A   A fall in the birth rate

   B   A fall in the death rate

   C   Net emigration

   D   Net immigration   [1]

4   What is meant by 'overpopulation'?

   A   There is a high geographical density of population

   B   There is a high population relative to the available area of cultivatable land

   C   There is a high population relative to the economic resources available

   D   There is net immigration   [1]

5   What is most likely to cause an increase in the birth rate?

   A   A fall in state pensions

   B   A fall in government spending on primary education

   C   A rise in the cost of living

   D   A rise in the proportion of females going to university   [1]

Total: [5]

> Chapter 32

Differences in economic development between countries

LEARNING INTENTION

By the end of this chapter, you will be able to:

- discuss the causes of economic development between countries
- explain the consequences of differences in economic development between countries.

KEY TERMS

economic development   investment   productivity

primary sector   secondary sector   tertiary sector

Key skills activities

1. For each of countries, A–D, shown in Table 32.1, explain why the characteristic identified may **not** mean that the country has a low level of economic development. Write your reasons in your notebook.

Table 32.1: Level of economic development

	Below the global average number of hospital beds per 1 000 of population	Above the global average population growth	Above the average size of the primary sector	Below the average number of university students
Country A	✓			
Country B		✓		
Country C			✓	
Country D				✓

TIP

Remember that while economic growth and economic development can be linked, they do not always move in the same direction.

32 Differences in economic development between countries

2. A very high level of economic development can reinforce future economic development. Similarly, a low level of economic development can reinforce that level. It can be difficult for a country to break out of a circle of low-level development. Figure 32.1 shows how low emigration of skilled workers can lead to further emigration of skilled workers.

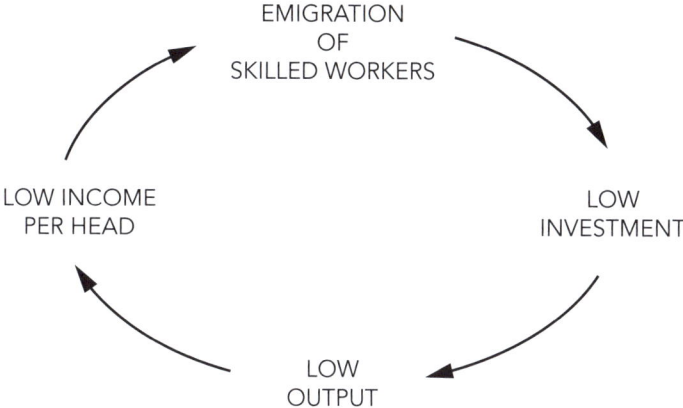

Figure 32.1: Emigration of skilled workers

Complete the following diagrams.

a

b

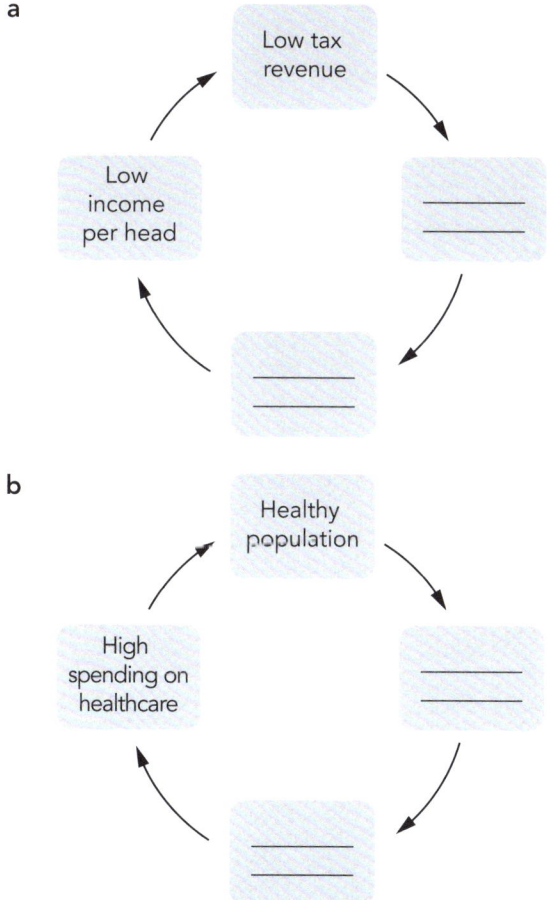

> **SELF-ASSESSMENT**
>
> How confident did you feel completing Activity 2? Think about the points below. Then circle the number of smiley faces to show your level of confidence from 1 (need to revisit my understanding of economic development) to 5 (feeling very confident).
>
> - Do you know the difference between economic growth and economic development?
> - Do you know the key influences on economic development?
>
>

3   Produce a poster on how increasing economic sustainability can raise the level of a country's economic development.

Chapter 32 practice questions

Circle the correct answer to each question.

1   What impact would economic development have on adult illiteracy, infant mortality and life expectancy?

	Adult illiteracy	Infant mortality	Life expectancy
A	decrease	decrease	increase
B	increase	decrease	decrease
C	increase	increase	decrease
D	decrease	increase	increase

[1]

2   As an economy develops, what usually happens to the population of workers employed in the primary and tertiary sectors?

	Primary	Tertiary
A	decrease	decrease
B	decrease	increase
C	increase	increase
D	increase	decrease

[1]

3   What is an indicator of low economic development?

    A   Lack of malnutrition

    B   Lack of sanitation

    C   Low inflation rate

    D   Low population growth rate [1]

4   According to the United Nations, a country is classified as having very high development when it achieves an HDI value above:

    A   0.6

    B   0.7

    C   0.8

    D   0.9 [1]

5   What would be most likely to promote both economic growth and economic development?

    A   Improved healthcare

    B   Increased interest rate

    C   Lower school-leaving age

    D   Shorter holidays for workers [1]

Total: [5]

Section 5 practice questions

1   Read the source material carefully before answering all parts of the question.

Guinea-Bissau fact file	2022
Population	2.06m
Life expectancy	63 years (m/f)
Employment in agriculture	68%
Urban population with access to drinking water	36%

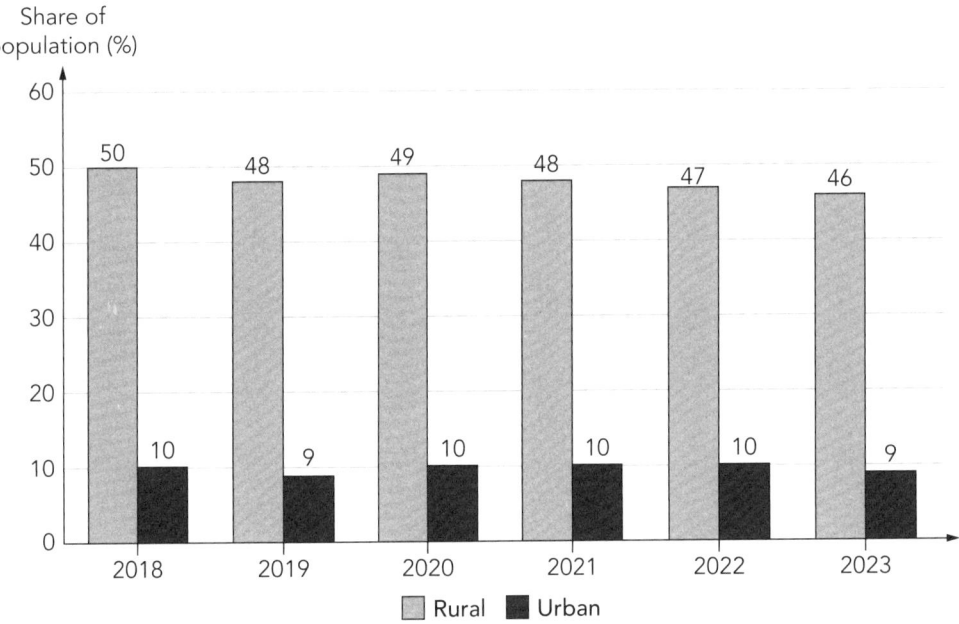

Figure 1: Share of population living in extreme poverty in Africa in rural and urban areas, 2018–2023

Figure 1 shows the share of the population living in extreme poverty in Africa. It indicates that there are clear differences between urban and rural areas. The reality is that the poorest in West Africa are undernourished and lack access to basic services such as electricity and safe drinking water. People on the lowest incomes usually have even less access to education and community healthcare than those living elsewhere in Africa.

West Africa has some of the poorest countries in the world. In 2022, all of the countries shown in Table 1 had a percentage of population living in 'extreme poverty' above the African average of 6.8%.

Table 1: Extreme poverty and living standards in West Africa, 2022

Country	Population (m)	Population living in extreme poverty^ (m)	Real GDP per head $	HDI value*
Côte d'Ivoire	27.5	2.1 (7.6%)	2 486	0.550
Ghana	32.8	6.9 (21.0%)	2 204	0.632
Guinea-Bissau	2.06	0.5 (24.3%)	776	0.483
Guinea	13.5	1.3 (9.6%)	1 515	0.465
Liberia	5.2	1.8 (34.6%)	754	0.487
Mauritania	4.6	0.3 (5.6%)	2 065	0.556
Senegal	16.9	1.3 (7.7%)	1 599	0.511
Sierra Leone	8.4	1.1 (See Question (a))	476	0.477

^Estimate *Latest data

Measuring living standards is a complex process due to the many variables involved. The most common measure, real GDP per head, is used by most countries and non-government organisations. Another measure is the composite Human Development Index (HDI) which takes a wider view of measuring living standards. All countries shown in Table 1 are grouped under 'low human development'. It should be remembered that neither of these measures is particularly accurate; it is more of a guide due to the problems of measuring economic variables in poor countries.

Refer to the information in the source material in your answers.

a Calculate the percentage population in Sierra Leone living in extreme poverty. [2]

b Identify **two** components of the Human Development Index. [2]

c Explain why extreme poverty in Africa is higher in rural areas than in urban areas. [2]

d Explain **two** policies that might reduce poverty in West Africa. [4]

e Analyse the relationship between real GDP per head and the Human Development Index for the countries shown in Table 1. [4]

f Discuss whether or not real GDP per head is the best way of comparing living standards between countries in West Africa. [6]

Total: [20]

> **TIP**
>
> Try to give an accurate answer as the components are specific.

Improve this answer

Here is a sample answer to part e:

GDP per head and the HDI are measures of living standards. Both measures have an income component, although HDI includes two other things as well. It makes the HDI more accurate.

You would expect the two to be closely related. At the top end, this is true. Côte d'Ivoire has the highest GDP per head and a high HDI score. There is a strong relationship for Ghana. At the bottom, Sierra Leone has the lowest GDP per head and the second lowest HDI measure.

> **YOUR CHALLENGE**
>
> See whether you can improve this answer. Before you write your answer, think about the points below:
>
> - The early reference to HDI can be improved by giving details of the other two components.
> - The data analysis is sound but should make some reference to the less clear relationships for Guinea and Liberia.
> - The answer would benefit from a final sentence noting whether the relationship is strong (or not), and the extent to which the data is accurate.

> **TIP**
>
> Before writing this answer, it will be helpful to rank the country's GDP per head and HDI values in numerical order, starting with 1 for the highest and 8 for the lowest.

2   Within the European Union, Ireland has experienced a remarkable period of economic development. Real GDP per head has continued to increase even during the COVID-19 pandemic. Much of the growth has come from Ireland's low-tax policy of attracting foreign-owned companies in financial services, Big Tech (the most influential companies in IT) and scientific research. This growth has transformed the structure of Ireland's economy.

   a   Define 'economic development'. [2]

   b   Explain why changes in real GDP per head are widely used as a measure of economic development. [4]

   c   Analyse why an economy that has real GDP per head twice that of another economy may not have living standards that are twice that of the other economy. [6]

   d   Discuss how the relative importance of primary, secondary and tertiary sectors in an economy changes with economic development. [8]

   Total: [20]

WORKED EXAMPLE ANSWER FOR PART D

The process of structural change affects all economies as they develop. The starting point is with the primary sector. Activities such as agriculture, mining and fishing traditionally form the base of such economies. The normal next stage is for a secondary sector to emerge to include processing raw materials and making some consumer goods. Often these are textiles and clothing which can be exported to high-income countries. The third stage is for a tertiary sector to develop. Its purpose is to provide a range of services such as banking, insurance and business services plus retail to support other parts of the economy.

Ireland is now a high-income country. Its economy has been transformed from one dependent on farming and food processing into a leading international business, technology and financial hub. Many US, European and Asian companies have chosen Ireland for their European base. It is an exceptional example. Not all economies move from primary due to the many obstacles in the path for their development.

3 Read the source material carefully before answering all parts of the question.

Australia fact file	2022
Population	25.7m
Real GDP per head	$51 720
Life expectancy	83.2 years
Net overseas migration (after lifting restriction)	408 000

Table 2: Population structures of Australia and Nigeria in 2022

Age group (years)	Australia %	Nigeria %
Under 10	12.0	30.4
10–19	11.0	23.4
20–29	13.6	16.2
30–59	39.9	25.1
60–79	24.2	6.7
80+	5.9	0.7

The population structure of Nigeria shown in Table 2 is typical of that for an economy with a relatively low level of development. Around 30% of the population is under ten years old. Nigeria had the highest birth rate of 36 in 2022. Nigeria also has a rapidly increasing population. In 2022, this was over

210 million with an average growth rate of 2.4% per year. Where living standards are low, as for the majority of Nigeria's population, children help parents in earning a living. An increase in the number of children can often result in an increase in household income.

The contrast with Australia is clear. There were relatively fewer young people, but more older people compared to Nigeria. Australia's birth rate was just 12 in 2022, way below the level needed to replace its population. For many years, the Australian government has had a fixation on immigration to meet the shortfall in its optimum population. Immigration has been necessary for its governments to pursue economic growth as the principal objective of its macroeconomic policy.

For the past 50 years, Australia has had annual net migration from the rest of the world, including Nigeria. The number of migrants from Nigeria has been small, typically around 1000 a year. In 2021 there were no migrants due to COVID-19 restrictions. When the block on migrants was released numbers increased to around 1600 and 2400 in 2022 and 2023. Australia has a strict working visa system which favours skilled workers and those able to bring business experience and investment into the country.

Refer to the information in the source material in your answers.

- **a** Calculate the difference in the percentage of the population under 20 years between Nigeria and Australia. **[2]**
- **b** Identify **two** reasons for the falling birth rate in Australia. **[2]**
- **c** Explain **one** reason why Australia has a higher percentage of its population aged 60 years and over compared to Nigeria. **[2]**
- **d** Explain **two** consequences of an ageing population in Australia. **[4]**
- **e** Analyse the effect on output and prices of an increase in the number of Nigerian migrants moving to Australia. **[4]**
- **f** Discuss whether or not immigration is the best way of promoting the development of Australia's economy. **[6]**

Total: **[20]**

> **TIP**
> The consequences for Australia are the same as for any other high-income country that you have studied.

WORKED EXAMPLE ANSWER FOR PART F

According to the source data, Australia has a long history of receiving migrants from the rest of the world. Migration increases the stock of labour, one of the factors of production. The long-run supply of labour increases which is necessary as Australia is experiencing a shortage of labour. The concern is that a shortage of labour will hold back Australia's economic development. As well as increasing the quantity of labour, the Australian government has been keen to improve the quality of labour through regulating which workers are eligible for a work visa. It seems that migrant workers from Nigeria will have special skills that are in short supply in Australia.

Section 5 practice questions

The use of migrant labour is not popular among many Australians. There is a view that migrants take jobs previously held by Australians and that earnings in some occupations are reduced as more migrants are employed. It is for these reasons that other policies could be used to promote Australia's economic development. One such policy is supply-side policy. If effective, this policy will increase total supply in the economy, prompting a rise in output. An important part of supply-side policy is to allocate resources to labour upskilling. This policy provides for the retraining of workers through educational or vocational programmes. It is effective where low skilled workers are given an opportunity to acquire new skills that make them more productive. Another relevant policy is to look at how investment by firms can be increased as a way of increasing total supply and productive potential.

Migration and supply-side policies can both be used to promote Australia's economic development. It is difficult to say which is likely to be most effective. It is likely that a combination of both may be needed.

4   In 2023, apart from Syria, all countries with the highest population growth rate were in Africa. These countries included South Sudan, Angola, Niger and Mali. In contrast, all countries experiencing a loss of population were in Europe. For countries such as Latvia, Croatia, Greece and Portugal, a combination of fewer births and emigration accounted for the decline. The extent of population decline though was much less than the increased growth in African countries.

> **TIP**
>
> You could use a simple optimum population diagram in your answer.

   a   Define 'optimum population'. [2]

   b   Explain the difference between an overpopulated and underpopulated economy. [4]

   c   Analyse the benefits of an increasing population in an economy. [6]

   d   Discuss whether or not a reduction in the size of the population has a negative effect on an economy. [8]

   Total: [20]

Improve this answer

Here is an answer to part c:

The population of a country is one of the four factors of production. In principle, an increasing population should produce more output. Firms can benefit from economies of scale and specialisation as the market for their products is bigger. As well as quantity of labour, the quality of labour should also be considered. For example ...

> **YOUR CHALLENGE**
>
> See whether you can improve this answer. Before you write your answer, think about the points below:
>
> - The answer is too brief. What is written is sound but the reference to quality of labour, which is important, needs to be extended to include an explanation. Before this, the point about economies of scale should be explained as it is not obvious.
> - There is no mention or explanation as to how an increase in tax revenue might be generated in an economy with an increasing population.
> - A final point to be made is that the benefits depend on the level of development of the economy.

Section 6
International trade and globalisation

Chapter 33
Specialisation and free trade

> **LEARNING INTENTIONS**
>
> By the end of this chapter, you will be able to:
> - define specialisation by country
> - analyse the basis for specialisation by country in terms of best resource allocation and/or lowest-cost production
> - discuss the advantages and disadvantages of specialisation
> - define free trade
> - discuss the advantages and disadvantages of free trade.

KEY TERMS	
free trade	specialisation by country

> **TIP**
>
> In examining how specialisation affects an economy, it is useful to consider the effects it may have on the government's macroeconomic aims.

Key skills activities

1. Decide in each case whether the following are reasons for Country X to specialise in banking and for Country Y to specialise in tea production. Complete Table 33.1 and include an explanation for each.

Table 33.1: Reasons for specialisation

Banking	Yes/no	Explanation
Good range of financial institutions		
Highly qualified labour force		
High-speed internet connections		
Tea production		
High labour costs		
High labour supply		
Suitable climate (warm with high humidity)		

33 Specialisation and free trade

 2 Download the diagram from GO (Worksheet 33.2) and complete it to show how opening up to free trade may affect consumers. The diagram shows how the size of a market increases when a country engages in free trade.

 3 Download the mind map from GO (Worksheet 33.3) and complete it to summarise some of the advantages and disadvantages that firms may experience from free trade.

> **SELF-ASSESSMENT**
>
> How confident did you feel completing Activity 3? Think about the points below. Then circle the medal you would award yourself.
>
> - Can you explain how productivity influences what a country may decide to specialise in?
>
> - Are you able to explain two reasons why a country with large deposits of coal may decide not to specialise in coal production?
>
>  Gold: Strong understanding – able to be a coach, that is able to explain the topic to another student
>
>  Silver: Good understanding – but stronger understanding of some aspects of the topic needed to reach gold standard
>
>  Bronze: Some understanding – but need to review most aspects of the topic

Chapter 33 practice questions

Circle the correct answer to each question.

1 What is a benefit to the global economy of countries specialising?

   A Higher output

   B Higher transport cost

   C Lower international trade

   D Lower mobility of resources   [1]

2 Which workers are most likely to suffer as a result of countries specialising?

   A Occupationally immobile workers

   B Private sector workers

   C Skilled workers

   D Young workers   [1]

3 What would indicate that a country should specialise in producing solar panels?

    A High demand for fossil fuels

    B High supply of fossil fuels

    C Low cost of producing solar panels

    D Low profit earned from producing solar panels   [1]

4 Free trade involves products being exchanged

    A which have no opportunity cost.

    B with no prices attached.

    C without any restrictions.

    D without any transport costs.   [1]

5 What is a possible disadvantage of a country deciding to specialise in a product it is good at producing?

    A Deficit on the current account of the balance of payments

    B Negative economic growth

    C Rise in the price level

    D Structural unemployment   [1]

Total: [5]

> Chapter 34
Globalisation and trade restrictions

LEARNING INTENTIONS

By the end of this chapter, you will be able to:

- define globalisation
- explain the causes and consequences of changes in globalisation
- explain the role of multinational companies (MNCs)
- explain the types of trade restrictions/methods of protection: tariffs, import quotas, subsidies and embargoes
- discuss the reasons for trade restrictions
- discuss the consequences of trade restrictions.

KEY TERMS

declining (sunset) industries   dumping   embargo

globalisation   infant (sunrise) industries

multinational company (MNC)   quota   subsidy

strategic industries   tariff   trade war

Key skills activities

1. You are the chief executive of a large multinational company producing a popular high-energy drink. You want to open a new factory producing and selling the drink in another country. Based on the information given in Table 34.1 about Countries A–D, decide which country you would select to build the factory. Write up the reasons for your selection in your notebook.

Table 34.1: Information on different countries

	Country A	Country B	Country C	Country D
Size of population	10m	30m	40m	50m
Indirect tax rate on soft drinks	20%	20%	15%	10%
Supply of skilled labour	High	Medium	Medium	Low
Corporate tax rate	15%	10%	10%	10%
Average income	$40 000	$30 000	$20 000	$10 000
Planning restrictions	High	High	Low	Low
Number of other high-energy drinks firms operating in the country	0	1	4	2
Economic growth rate	1%	5%	8%	4%

2   Collect ten labels from ten products with a country of origin on it that your family has purchased. Note how many countries the products have come from.

   a   What evidence do the products provide of globalisation?

   b   Do you think any of the countries you have found have particular advantages in producing the products?

   Write your answers in your notebook.

3   A government imposes a tariff on electric vehicles produced in other countries to support its infant electric vehicle industry. Decide whether each of the scenarios shown in Table 34.2 will be likely to decrease or increase the chances of the tariff being successful in promoting the growth of the infant industry. Complete Table 34.2 and include a reason for each decision.

Table 34.2: Scenarios affecting the success of a tariff in promoting the growth of an infant industry

Scenario	Decrease/ increase	Reason
Foreign governments retaliate with tariffs on the country's exports of electric vehicles.		
Inelastic demand for foreign electric vehicles.		
Reduced competition removes pressure on the infant industry to lower average cost.		
Some of the tariff revenue is used to subsidise the infant industry's purchase of capital equipment.		
There are significant economies of scale in the industry.		

34 Globalisation and trade restrictions

4 Place the 16 words/phrases in the word cloud into four groups of four connected words and state how they are connected. Some words/phrases may fit into more than one group. However, there is only one solution that will give four groups of connected words. Complete the grid below.

Dumping	Current account deficit	Embargo
Infant	Quota	Raise prices	Raise tax revenue
Reduce competition	Reduce choice	Reduce quality
Strategic	Sunrise	Sunset	Subsidy
Tariff	Unfair competition		

Word group				Connection

5 Produce a presentation on whether you think your government should increase or decrease trade restrictions.

> **TIP**
>
> Remember, a tariff is a tax on imports or exports, whereas a quota is a limit on imports or exports.

> **SELF-ASSESSMENT**
>
> How confident did you feel completing Activity 5? Think about the points below.
>
> - Can you explain how an increase in trade restrictions are stronger than others?
> - Do you understand that some arguments for imposing trade restrictions are stronger than others?
>
> Produce a revision card on the arguments for and against trade restrictions.

Chapter 34 practice questions

Circle the correct answer to each question.

1 What is meant by 'dumping'?

   A   The employment of cheap labour

   B   The imposition of tariffs on imports

   C   The removal of health and safety standards

   D   The sale of products below cost price in another country   [1]

2 Which change would increase the level of protection to domestic industries?

   A   A reduction in income tax

   B   A reduction in quota levels

   C   A reduction in subsidies to domestic producers

   D   A reduction in tariffs   [1]

3 The Vietnamese government decides to increase tariffs on imported buses. Which two groups in Vietnam may benefit from this decision?

   A   Bus passengers and the government

   B   Bus-producing companies and bus travel companies

   C   Bus travel companies and bus passengers

   D   The government and bus-producing companies   [1]

4 What is a reason for a government imposing an export tariff?

   A   To prevent prices rising in the country

   B   To prevent the country's unemployment rate rising

   C   To reduce a deficit on the current account of the balance of payments

   D   To reduce the competition faced by the country's firms   [1]

5 A good that is imported has perfectly inelastic demand and 500 units are sold in the country each month. If an embargo is placed on the import of the good, what will be the new annual sales in the country?

   A   0

   B   500

   C   1 000

   D   6 000   [1]

Total: [5]

Chapter 35
Foreign exchange rates

LEARNING INTENTIONS

By the end of this chapter, you will be able to:

- define foreign exchange rate
- explain the reasons for buying and selling foreign currencies
- analyse how a foreign exchange rate is determined in foreign exchange markets
- discuss the consequences of changes in foreign exchange rates.

KEY TERMS

appreciation   depreciation   floating exchange rate

foreign direct investment (FDI)   foreign exchange rate

hot money flows   workers' remittances

Key skills activities

1 Calculate:

  a An Indian product has a price of 360 rupees. The exchange rate is $1 = 90 Indian rupees. How much will the product sell for in dollars?

  b The exchange rate between the UK pound (£) and the dollar is £1 = $1.2. If a UK firm earns $18m from exporting a product, how much will its revenue be in UK £?

  c If the value of the dollar changes from $1 = 20 Mexican pesos to $1 = 22.8 Mexican pesos, what is the percentage rise in the value/price of the dollar?

  d What is a dollar worth in Brazilian real if US exports of $70m sell for 490m real?

Now, use your answers to match the figures with the letters in the grid to find the name of a Southeast Asian currency.

1	2	3	4	5	6	7	8	9	10	11	12	13
A	B	C	D	E	F	G	H	I	J	K	L	M
14	15	16	17	18	19	20	21	22	23	24	25	26
N	O	P	Q	R	S	T	U	V	W	X	Y	Z

Currency: ....

2   In each of the scenarios given in Table 35.1, decide whether those identified would benefit from an appreciation of the Australian dollar. Complete Table 35.1 and include an explanation for your decision in each case.

Table 35.1: The effects of an appreciation in the Australian dollar

Scenario	Benefit? Yes/no	Explanation
Chinese firms that sell goods to Australia		
Indian MNC that sends profits back to India		
Indonesians going on holiday to Australia		
Japanese firms that buy Australian food to sell in their shops		
Pakistani firms that compete with Australian firms in selling office equipment		
People from Greece who work in Australia and send money home to their relatives		
Thai speculators who have bought Australian dollars		

> **TIP**
>
> Remember that an export from one country is an import to another country. So, for example, an export from Australia to Sri Lanka will be an Australian export and a Sri Lankan import.

3 The mind map in Figure 35.1 is based on a rise in the value of a floating exchange rate. Draw a similar diagram based on a fall in the value of a floating exchange rate. Write your answer in your notebook or on a separate sheet of paper.

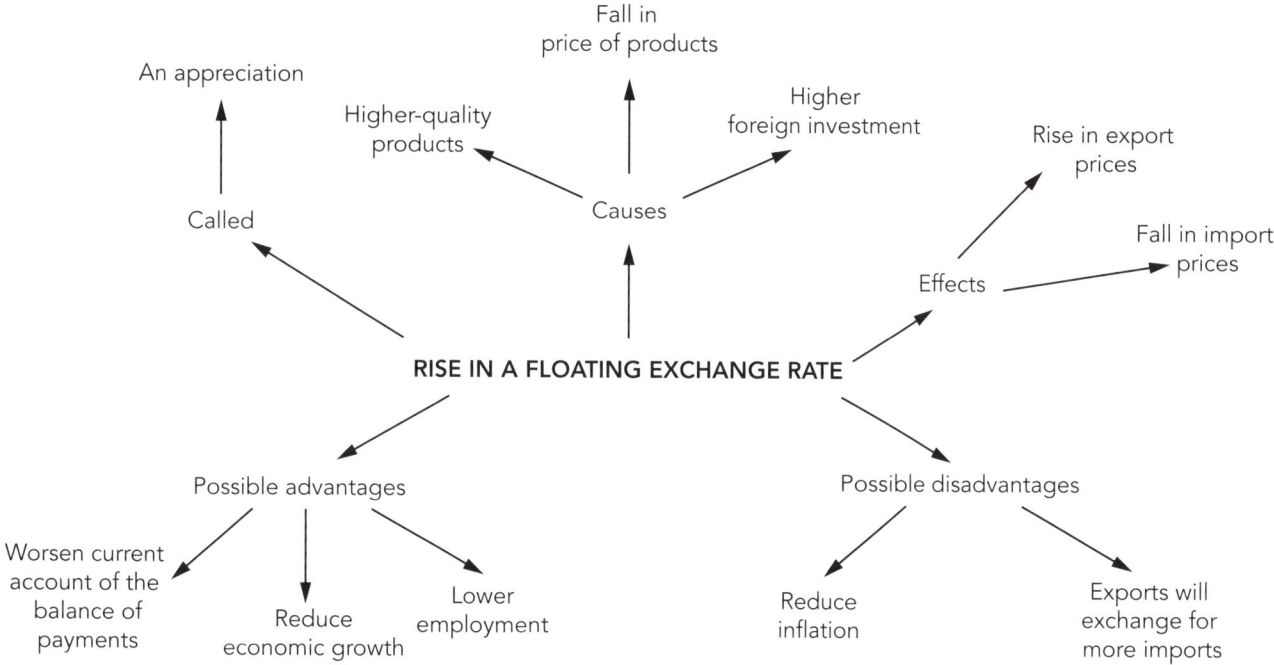

Figure 35.1: Rise in floating exchange rate

> ### SELF-ASSESSMENT
>
> How confident did you feel completing Activity 3? Think about the points below.
>
> - Can you identify how a change in the foreign exchange rate will affect export and import prices?
> - Are you able to explain how a change in the foreign exchange rate may affect a government's macroeconomic aims?
>
> Produce a poster on the causes and consequences of a change in foreign exchange rates. The poster could include two diagrams showing how the market for two currencies would be affected by, for example, a rise in the quality of one of the two country's exports.

4 Download the flowchart from GO (Worksheet 35.4) and complete it to show how a rise in incomes in Egypt is likely to affect the price of the South African rand and the price of South Africa's exports and imports.

5 Using the internet or the exchange rates table in the business section of a (It could be published in a regional newspaper as well?) newspaper, select three different currencies. Enter the value of the current exchange rate in the table. Check the exchange rates in two weeks' time and enter the new exchange rates. What has happened to the value of the currencies? Include a reason for the change in each exchange rate.

Currency	Current exchange rate	New exchange rate	Reason

Chapter 35 practice questions

Circle the correct answer to each question.

1 A fall in the exchange rate reduces a current account deficit. What could explain this?

   A   Export prices falling by less than export volume rises

   B   Export prices rising by more than export volume falls

   C   Import prices rising and import volume remaining unchanged

   D   Import prices rising by more than import volume falls [1]

2 Which change would cause the value of the US dollar to rise?

   A   US inflation rate rising more rapidly than other countries' inflation rates

   B   US interest rates rising

   C   US firms buying firms in foreign countries

   D   US tourists spending more abroad [1]

3 What would cause China to earn more dollars?

   A   Chinese airlines transporting US citizens to the US

   B   Chinese tourists visiting the US

   C   Payment of interest to a US bank on a loan to a Chinese firm

   D   Payment to a Chinese firm by the Chinese government [1]

> **TIP**
>
> A change in an exchange rate affects both the price and value of the currency. For example, a rise in the exchange rate of Bangladesh would mean that each taka would buy more of another currency and the price of the taka in other currencies would increase.

35 Foreign exchange rates

4 What is the most likely reason why a government would encourage a rise in its country's foreign exchange rate?

　A　To encourage economic growth

　B　To increase employment

　C　To reduce a deficit on the current account of the balance of payments

　D　To reduce inflation [1]

5 How may a country avoid an upward movement in its exchange rate?

　A　A reduction in public sector pay

　B　A rise in personal income tax rates

　C　The imposition of tariffs on imports

　D　The sale of the domestic currency [1]

Total: [5]

> Chapter 36

Current account of the balance of payments

LEARNING INTENTIONS

By the end of this chapter, you will be able to:

- describe the components of the current account of the balance of payments
- calculate deficits and surpluses on the current account of the balance of payments
- analyse the causes for current account deficits and surpluses
- analyse the consequences of current account deficits and surpluses
- discuss the range of policies available to achieve balance of payments stability and their effectiveness.

KEY TERMS

balance of payments	current account balance	primary income
secondary income	trade in goods	trade in goods deficit
trade in goods surplus	trade in services	trade in services surplus

Key skills activities

1 Calculate:

   a A country's trade in goods if its exports are $320m and its imports are $429m

   b A country's trade in goods and services balance if its exports of goods are $720m, imports of goods are $550m, exports of services are $150m and imports of services are $125m c   A country's current account balance if exports of goods are $330m, imports of goods are $310m, exports of services are $800m, imports of services are $617m, primary income is $85m and secondary income is −$57m

d   A country's primary income balance if credits on the primary income balance are $102m and debits on the primary income balance are $140m.

Add the answers you have calculated to find a figure that is the same as the population in 2024 of a country that had a current account deficit of $1.3bn in the fourth quarter of 2023.

Total: .... Country: ....

SELF-ASSESSMENT

How confident did you feel completing Activity 1? Think about the points below. Then circle the medal you would award yourself.

- Do you know what to include in your calculation of current account debits and surpluses?

- Do you know what may cause a current account deficit and what its consequences may be?

Gold: Strong understanding – able to be a coach, that is able to explain the topic to another student

Silver: Good understanding – but stronger understanding of some aspects of the topic needed to reach gold standard

Bronze: Some understanding – but need to review most aspects of the topic

2   A government may or may not consider that it needs to take action to reduce a current account deficit. It will depend largely on the cause of the current account deficit. For each of the causes of the current account deficit shown in Table 36.1, decide whether government action is or is not needed. Complete Table 36.1 with a reason in each case.

Table 36.1: Whether government action is needed to reduce a current account deficit

Cause of current account deficit	Government action needed/not needed	Reason
Fall in incomes abroad		
Fall in productivity		
Rise in expenditure on capital goods		
Rise in expenditure on raw materials		
Rise in inflation rate		
Trade restrictions imposed by foreign governments		

TIP

Be careful not to confuse a current account deficit and a government budget deficit.

3   Figure 36.1 shows the causes, consequences and policy measures required to reduce a current account surplus. Draw a similar diagram identifying the causes, consequences and policy measures to reduce a current account deficit. Write your answer in your notebook or on a separate sheet of paper.

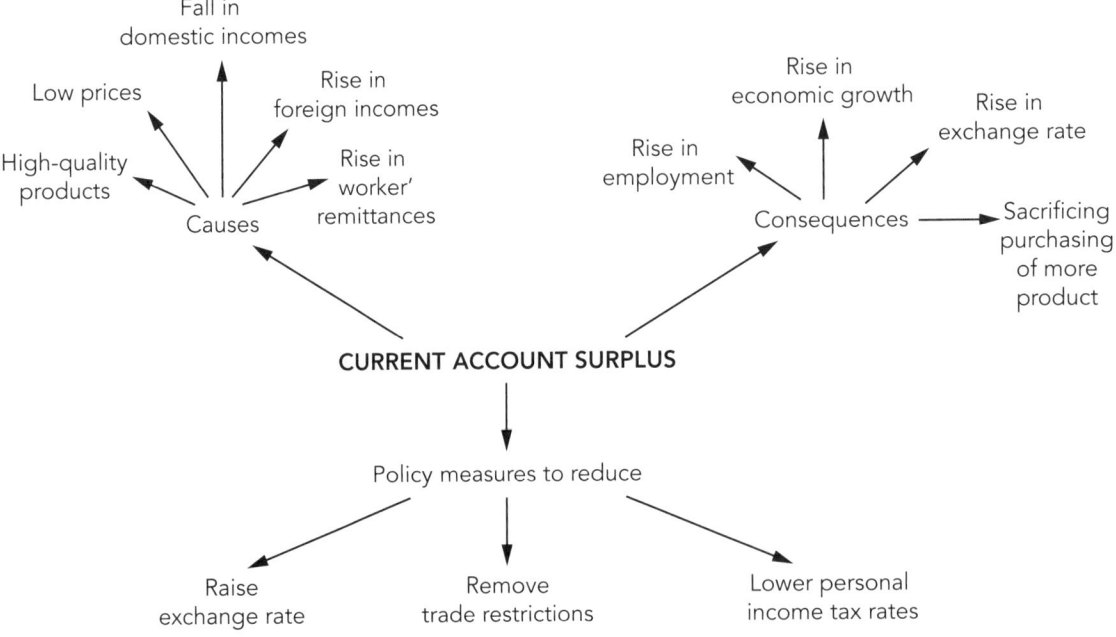

Figure 36.1: Current account surplus

36 Current account of the balance of payments

 4 Download the crossword grid from GO (Worksheet 36.4) and complete it using the clues below.

Across

1 Part of the balance of payments. (7, 7)

7 Term for an item that brings money into the country. (6)

8 What is likely to happen to a country's foreign exchange rate if there is a current account surplus. (4)

10 Second section of the current account of the balance of payments. (5, 2, 8)

12 The number of sections of the current account of the balance of payments. (4)

13 The currency of Peru. (3)

14 What will be reduced if there is a current account deficit. (6)

16 Do governments usually try to achieve balance of payments stability? (3)

17 What balance of payments stability is for a government. (3)

20 The fourth section of the current account of the balance of payments. (9, 5)

22 This is one influence on how significant a current account deficit may be. (4)

23 The third section of the current account of the balance of payments. (7, 6)

25 A situation which may reduce imports. (9)

26 Goods and services bought from other countries. (7)

Down

1 Payments received from economic transactions with other countries exceed payments made to other countries. (7, 7, 7)

2 What the current account can be said to be in when it is in deficit. (3)

3 First section of the current account of the balance of payments. (5, 2, 5)

4 A rise in these may cause a change in a country's current account balance. (6)

5 What may be given to domestic firms to increase their exports. (7)

6 Objectives a government will have for the macroeconomy. (4)

9 Goods and services sold to other countries. (7)

11 What may be increased as a result of a current account surplus. (10)

15 What may occur, in terms of the foreign exchange rate, if there is a current account deficit. (12)

18 When foreigners make these when buying imports, they are included in the current account. (8)

19 What an economy may do if there is a current account surplus. (4)

21 What the current account is in if the value of debit items exceeds that of the value of credit items. (7)

24 The current account figure will be this if the value of debit items exceeds that of the value of credit items. (5)

Chapter 36 practice questions

Circle the correct answer to each question.

1   Which is an item that would appear in the trade in services component of the balance of payments?

   A   Books

   B   Paper

   C   Printing presses

   D   Royalty payments (payments to authors) [1]

2   What would increase the debits on a country's trade in goods and services?

   A   A foreign firm investing in the country

   B   Domestic firms buy more imported raw materials

   C   Domestic insurance companies sell more policies to foreign residents

   D   The government receiving a loan from a foreign bank [1]

3   Which change may reduce a country's current account deficit?

   A   An increase in the country's inflation rate

   B   An increase in the quality of imports

   C   A rise in incomes abroad

   D   A rise in the exchange rate [1]

4   In which section of the current account of the balance of payments would interest paid on a loan from a foreign bank appear?

   A   Primary income

   B   Secondary income

   C   Trade in goods

   D   Trade in services [1]

5   What items appear in the secondary income section of the current account of the balance of payments?

   A   Exports and imports of goods below a value of $100

   B   Exports and imports of raw materials used in the secondary sector

   C   Those that relate to investment income earned from and paid to other countries

   D   Those which are given to and received from other countries not in return for producing a good or service [1]

   Total: [5]

Section 6 practice questions

1   Read the source material carefully before answering all parts of the question.

Malaysia fact file	2023
Population	33.6m
Unemployment rate	3.3%
Real GDP per head	$12 470
Growth of GDP	4.9%
Current account surplus	1.2% GDP
Food imported	60%

The foreign exchange rate of the ringgit, Malaysia's currency, is determined freely by supply and demand. In early 2024, the ringgit's value hit a 26-year low against the US dollar. Figure 1 shows this depreciation.

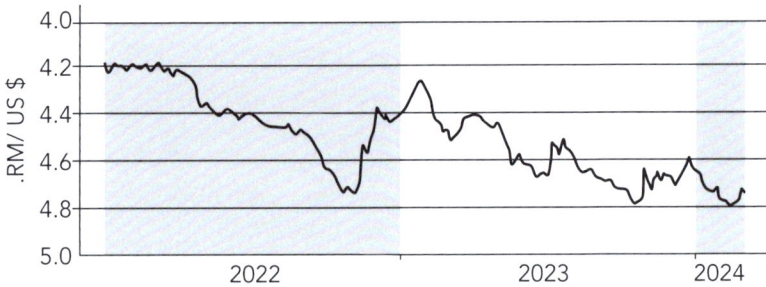

Figure 1: Ringgit–US dollar exchange rate, 2022–2024

> **TIP**
>
> Note that the scale on the y-axis has been turned upside down. This makes the depreciation clear.

Malaysia's central bank responded to this latest depreciation by selling some of its reserves of dollars in order to stabilise the currency. The government was not unduly concerned about the fall as Malaysia's economy was improving following the shock of the COVID-19 pandemic.

A particular concern of the government though was the impact of the ringgit's depreciation on consumers. The rate of inflation in 2023 was 1.8% but forecast to rise to 3.3% in 2024. A weaker ringgit increases the cost of imported food, which is mainly sourced from China, Thailand and Australia. The weak ringgit also raises the prices of manufactured goods that are dependent on imported raw materials as well as services such as transportation and restaurants.

The ringgit's continuing depreciation was not all bad news. On the contrary, it was good news for the tens of thousands of Malays working in Singapore. The weak ringgit makes Singapore an attractive place for Malays to work, either as temporary residents or as day workers. Remittances from such workers are a substantial contribution to Malaysia's current account surplus on the balance of payments.

Malaysia's government fears a 'talent drain'. There is already a lack of skilled labour, with many unemployed people lacking even basic skills. A recent report stated that many job applicants lacked the right technical skills required for the needs of Malaysia's job market. The report also commented on how a skills mismatch was largely responsible for the high rate of graduate unemployment.

Refer to the information in the source material in your answers.

- a Calculate the percentage change in the depreciation of the ringgit against the dollar in 2023. [2]
- b Identify where remittances made by Malaysian workers abroad are recorded in the current account of Malaysia's balance of payments. [2]
- c Explain why the depreciation of the ringgit is well received by Malay workers in Singapore. [2]
- d Explain two ways in which Malaysian consumers can expect to be harmed by the depreciation of the ringgit. [4]
- e Analyse the impact on output and the price level of a Chinese multinational company (MNC) choosing to relocate to Malaysia. [4]
- f Discuss whether or not the depreciation of the ringgit is having a positive impact on Malaysia's current account of the balance of payments. [6]

Total: [20]

WORKED EXAMPLE ANSWER FOR PART A

Looking at Figure 1:

Start of 2023: 4.4 ringgits to one dollar

End of 2023: 4.6 ringgits to one dollar

The ringgit has fallen by 0.2 ringgits against the dollar in 2023.

So, the percentage change is (0.2 ÷ 4.4) × 100%, which equals **4.55%**.

TIP

To avoid making a mistake, try to get a rough idea of the answer before doing the calculation.

2 The World Trade Organisation (WTO) aims to promote globalisation by ensuring that trade flows as smoothly and freely as possible with minimal restrictions. It oversees a global system of trade rules, settles trade disputes between members and supports the needs of developing economies. World trade volume and value has increased by an average of 4% and 6%, respectively, since the WTO was set up in 1995. Post-COVID-19, trade growth has fallen due to the impact of the pandemic and external geopolitical uncertainties.

- a Define 'globalisation'. [2]
- b Explain **two** reasons for the growth of global trade. [4]

c   Analyse the consequences of globalisation for consumers and producers. [6]

d   Discuss whether or not there are threats to the spread of globalisation. [8]

Total: [20]

> **TIP**
>
> You need to allow sufficient time to answer this 8-mark 'Discuss' question.

Improve this answer

Here is a sample answer to part d:

Globalisation is the process by which the economies of the world have become more linked to each other. Barriers to trade have been broken down as seen in the steady annual rate of growth in world trade.

Reducing transport costs is the key to increasing globalisation further. Where a product is physically made is now less important than it was due to economies of scale in transport. A second reason for globalisation has been the way in which advances in communications have made it easy for businesses to contact each other. This is the power of the internet. These reasons are still valid today and should help to sustain the continued growth of world trade.

The spread of globalisation was hit by the COVID-19 pandemic. Trade volumes fell and pressure built up on supply chains that were unable to meet consumer and producer needs. This threat was unexpected. Other threats have come from trading blocs like the African Continental Free Trade Area.

(Sorry Out of time)

> **YOUR CHALLENGE**
>
> See whether you can improve this answer. Before you write your answer, think about the points below:
>
> - The first paragraph is OK but is not strictly necessary.
> - The second paragraph makes clear how the spread of globalisation might continue.
> - The third paragraph starts well but as the student runs out of time, it has little content. There is scope to write about the threats such as the aftermath of COVID-19, global political disputes and trade disputes between China and the USA.

3   Read the source material carefully before answering all parts of the question.

CPTPP fact file	2023
Population	515m
Share of global GDP	16%
Real GDP per head	$35 614
Share of world trade	26%

In 2023 the United Kingdom (UK) became the 12th member of the CPTPP (Comprehensive and Progressive Agreement for the Trans-Pacific Partnership) making this group the third largest in global trade after the US and China. The European Union, of which the UK was formally a member, was now fourth largest in terms of the value of exports and imports. Table 1 shows the UK's trade with four selected CPTPP members. The other members are Brunei Darassalam, Canada, Chile, Mexico, New Zealand, Peru and Vietnam.

Table 1: The UK trade in goods and services with CPTPP countries, 2022

	Exports		Imports	
	£ billion	%	£ billion	%
Australia	12.4	1.5	4.8	0.5
Japan	13.6	1.6	14.1	1.6
Malaysia	3.3	0.4	2.6	0.3
Singapore	13.6	1.6	7.1	0.8
Total	42.9	5.1	28.6	3.2

CPTPP members have a shared objective to make international trade as free from restrictions as possible. This is at odds with the EU's approach of protecting the interests of its member states from competition from outside the union. One benefit for the UK is that the tariff on whisky exports to Malaysia is reduced from 80% to 0%. Tariffs on car exports, currently 30%, will be gradually reduced, giving a boost to UK producers. A different benefit is that members will be able to enjoy freer trade in agricultural products from Canada, Australia and New Zealand, all of which are major food producers. This also improves the security of supplies for countries like the UK and Malaysia which rely heavily on food imports. These are just two examples of CPTPP membership making it cheaper and easier to trade. The UK government hopes that membership will lead to an expansion of exports to a group of countries that contains many of the world's emerging economies.

The economic principle behind the CPTPP is that of specialisation. Consumers gain through lower prices and more variety of goods and services. Producers gain the benefits of economies of scale through being able to trade tariff-free in a bigger market.

The early success of the CPTPP has led to applications for membership from countries in the Asia-Pacific rim, including from China. Economists are divided over whether China's membership would boost its economy at a time when its economic growth rate is falling or whether Chinese goods would swamp the less robust CPTPP members.

Refer to the information in the source material in your answers.

a Calculate the balance of the UK's trade with other CPTPP members and say whether the balance is in a surplus or deficit. [2]

b Identify which of the CPTPP countries trades relatively the most with the UK. [2]

c Explain what is meant by 'specialisation'. [2]

d Explain **two** reasons why the UK should benefit from CPTPP membership. [4]

e Analyse the impact on total demand and total supply of the UK joining the CPTPP. [4]

f Discuss whether or not the CPTPP should accept any new members. [6]

Total: [20]

Improve this answer

Here is a sample answer to part d:

The CPTPP operates on the principle of specialisation and free trade. Cutting tariffs on exports allows members to specialise in goods and services where they have an advantage over other members. The UK should benefit from providing financial services, especially to members in high-income countries. New markets are being opened up.

A second benefit is the removal or reduction in tariffs on food imports. In the case of the UK, these tariffs were imposed by the EU on non-members as a way of protecting its own farmers.

YOUR CHALLENGE

See whether you can improve this answer. Before you write your answer, think about the point below:

- Both benefits draw upon the source material and are to the point of the question. The second benefit especially could be elaborated with a little more economic analysis. No additional factual knowledge is assumed.

4 In 2023, India announced an embargo on the export of onions, an essential ingredient in Asian cooking. The decision came after a surge in domestic onion prices from around $12 to $18 per 100 kg bag. The ban followed record exports of onions to Bangladesh, Mauritius and Sri Lanka. Other restrictive measures that have been tried include minimum export prices and export duties, but these have failed to stabilise the market.

a Define a 'trade restriction'. [2]

b Explain **two** ways in which an embargo is restrictive. [4]

c Analyse why countries impose trade restrictions. [6]

d Discuss whether or not trade restrictions harm the economy of the country that imposes them. [8]

Total: [20]

WORKED EXAMPLE ANSWER FOR PART D

There are many forms of trade restriction. The most widely used are tariffs and quotas on imports and restrictions such as those applied by India to stop the export of onions.

There are many reasons why a country that imposes trade restrictions hopes to benefit. An obvious reason is to protect employment in infant, declining and strategic industries from unfair foreign competition. A related reason is to reduce the cost of imported goods on the current account of the balance of payments, usually when there is a trade deficit. Other reasons are to protect domestic firms from unfair practices such as dumping.

These restrictions may not always benefit the economy of the country that imposes them. It can be argued, for example, that infant and declining industries should be left to deal with competition in the market, provided the competition is fair. This is the best way to ensure an efficient allocation of resources for consumers. There is also the opportunity cost of the resources that has to be committed to retain them. In the case of dumping, a firm's production costs are lower than they should be. This makes it difficult for the firm to compete in a free market in the future and causes little incentive for manufacturers of clothing, footwear and vehicles, for example, to improve the quality of their products.